Runes:

A Guide To The Magic, Meanings, Spells, Divination & Rituals Of Runes

© **Copyright 2019 by Sofia Visconti - All rights reserved.**

This document is geared towards providing exact and reliable information in regards to the topic and issue covered. The publication is sold with the idea that the publisher is not required to render accounting, officially permitted or otherwise qualified services. If advice is necessary, legal or professional, a practiced individual in the profession should be ordered.

From a Declaration of Principles which was accepted and approved equally by a Committee of the American Bar Association and a Committee of Publishers and Associations.

In no way is it legal to reproduce, duplicate, or transmit any part of this document in either electronic means or in printed format. Recording of this publication is strictly prohibited, and any storage of this document is not allowed unless with written permission from the publisher. All rights reserved.

The information provided herein is stated to be truthful and consistent, in that any liability, in terms of inattention or otherwise, by any usage or abuse of any policies, processes, or directions contained within is the solitary and utter responsibility of the recipient reader. Under no circumstances will any legal responsibility or blame be held against the publisher for any reparation, damages, or monetary loss due to the information herein, either directly or indirectly.

Respective authors own all copyrights not held by the publisher.

The information herein is offered for informational purposes solely and is universal as so. The presentation of the information is without a contract or any type of guarantee assurance.

The trademarks that are used are without any consent, and the publication of the trademark is without permission or backing by the trademark owner. All trademarks and brands within this book are for clarifying purposes only and are owned by the owners themselves, not affiliated with this document.

Table of Contents

Introduction

Chapter One: Ancient Origins

Chapter Two: Understanding Runic Alphabets

Chapter Three: Spell Casting and Divining

Chapter Four: The New World

Chapter Five: Witness Your Future

Chapter Six: Runic Exercises & Preparing Your Mind

Chapter Seven: Rituals to Accompany the Study

Chapter Eight: Facts about the Blank Rune and Whether You Should Read It

Chapter Nine: Runic Spreads

Chapter Ten: Hidden Runic Roots

Chapter Eleven: Uncomfortable Truths about Norse Mythology

Chapter Twelve: Runes and Naming of the Seven Days of the Week

Chapter Thirteen: Runes and the Power Plants' Flowers

Chapter Fourteen: Going Deeper

Conclusion

Resources

Introduction

There is evidence that many people these days want to learn runes. However, because it's ancient, there is no clear guide on how to go about it. There are many misconceptions surrounding the topic of runes. Some associate them with magic, spells, and divination. On the other hand, some only know them as a sacred alphabet. All these are right, but depending on the context of the user. The starting point for anyone wishing to learn and use runes is to understand the whole topic. Runes have been there since ancient times, and like many other things, they have evolved over time.

Did you know that similar to Hebrew letters, each runic symbol has a meaning? Well, for your information, each symbol has, in fact, a deeper meaning that goes beyond its function as a letter. In a nutshell, runes are practical, effective, and useful symbols that have a wide array of uses. Just to shed more light on this interesting topic, today, some of the most common application of rune lore is in areas of spell casting and divination. Also, the modern-day, Bluetooth logo is a combination of two runes. What this means is that there is a lot to learn and understand about runes before one can successfully apply them.

This book delves into the topic of runes to bring out what they are and what they are not. It focuses on the history of runes, runic alphabet, spell casting and divining, modern use, connecting with the sources of energy and future, exercises and descriptions, and lastly, rituals to accompany the study. We provide details and uncover what many do not know about runes so that anyone interested can have an easy time learning the ropes of runes. We do this knowing that the real power of runes comes from understanding their value. More specifically, we get the real power of runes when we find the wisdom in each runic symbol and internalize it within ourselves.

While the contents of this book may seem overwhelming at first, you will find it easy and enjoyable learning about runes. This book is, therefore, intended to be a guide to anyone interested in learning runes, how to use them, and their benefits. What we know is that runes can only help you if you understand them better and you can practice. As you read, you will gain knowledge, and more importantly, understanding the power and usefulness of runes. If you get things right, you might reap a lot, including unlocking your potential to connect with sources of energy, healing, and love. As an inspiration, some people have mastered the art and are gaining from the hidden power of runes. You can become one of them too.

Every chapter of this book brings out interesting ideas you probably didn't know. For instance, one of the chapters of this book explains how you can see your future with the help of runes. It explains how you can use runes by sending them into the Cosmo to help you consult as well as manifest a goal about a given situation. We hope that this and other interesting things you learn in this book will be useful. Without further ado, let's delve into the deeper meaning of runes and their application.

Chapter One: Ancient Origins

The history of runes is very vital for your understanding and how you can apply them. While there are a lot of historical facts worth knowing about runes, this chapter provides a brief history of context only. Before you understand what it is and how it works, it is important to know how runes developed.

Runes have a history that dates back to about 100 BCE in Northern European and about 1600 CE in Scandinavian countries. While most runes came from Germanic tribes, a couple of others were stolen from Greeks and Romans as well. Since then, runes have evolved. However, the fact is that despite the changes that have occurred over time, they have been consistently used for centuries.

Initially, runes were characters in several alphabets of Germanic languages used in the first century. As Christianity spread, runes were gradually replaced with Latin letters. However, despite the replacement, runes did not completely disappear. Those who understood their deep meaning kept and continued using them. They were then reviewed in the twentieth century when many ancient spiritual practices were making a comeback. While a lot has been said about runes over time, the complete story remains unclear. For this reason, there is so much variation when it comes to symbols, meaning, and their uses.

Origins

Runes stemmed from an ancient form of the alphabet that was widely used by Nordic and Germanic tribes of Northern Europe, Britain, and Scandinavia. While their primary use was in writing, runes were also used those times for magical as well as divination purposes. Although their existence came to the limelight in the 3rd century, there is a belief that they existed long before that time.

According to Norse Mythology, the word rune derived from the German word run whose meaning is secret or whisper. It is further believed that the first person to gain the knowledge of runes was Odin, the king of gods. He gained it to help him in war and give him the wisdom to lead the other gods well. History has it that in order to gain full knowledge of runes, Odin hung himself in the Tree of life for nine days. When the period was over, he had acquired so much wisdom that helped him to understand that, indeed, hidden powers existed in runes.

Overjoyed with the fact that there was so much hidden power in runes, Odin shared the knowledge he had gained with humanity. From there, it spread, and it has also evolved over time to what it is currently. It is, however, unclear whether or not Odin was taught the signs, or he developed them just to make it easier for humankind to understand.

A couple of years later, the rise of Scandinavian and Viking languages around AD800 led to the replacement of a couple of runic signs and alphabets. This might explain the existence of the various types of runic alphabets and the many changes that have taken place over time. This is evidenced by the remains of carvings that were created at different times and are still kept for reference to date. In ancient times, runic signs were carved into hard surfaces, including wood, bone, metal, and stone, among others. As of the 21st century, there were still people who still curved runes into surfaces just like it was done in ancient times.

Early Inscriptions

Early runic inscriptions dating back to around 150 AD have been found in many objects, including stones, weapons, and jewelry, among others. While most of these objects vanished as those who made them underwent Christianization, some uses of runes, especially for specialized purposes withstood the wave of change and remained up until the 20th century. In Northern Europe and Rural Sweden, for instance, runes were able to resist the change and remained since they had a special place in calendars and decoration activities.

From 150 AD to around 1100 AD, there were three best-known alphabets, namely the Elder Futhark, the Anglo Saxon Futhorc, and the younger Futhark. While there are many other runic alphabets, they are also descendent from these three ancient ones. In fact, even the Latin alphabet bears a great resemblance to the Elder Futhark. Many argue that a lot of exchange and borrowing happened during the times when Christianity was spreading to many parts of Europe, especially in the Northern areas that saw a massive change from their old lifestyles and religions to the Christian way of life.

Norse Beliefs

Norse beliefs are embedded in the very rich Norse Mythology, which is often called the Germanic Mythology. But what is this mythology all about? Well, it is not just a myth but is also a religion practiced by the Vikings as well as the Germanic people. Vikings were conquerors, raiders, traders, settlers, and explorers from current-day Denmark, Iceland, Norway, and Sweden. These are the people who spread the Norse Mythology. While there are many beliefs in Norse Mythology, not all of them are explored in runes books and inscriptions that have helped hand over the beliefs from old generations to the modern-day.

One of the famous Norse beliefs is the argument that there is not one world but nine, perhaps corresponding to the nine planets. It is also worth noting that the concept of luck came from Norse beliefs. Essentially, there was no Norse code of conduct since morality was based on family bonds and a concept known as 'weird,' which meant fate or luck. Other beliefs included those of rebirth after death. Other beliefs, including the killing of men in raids with the belief that those killers would be rewarded. Some of these beliefs were swept away by the wave of Christianity, but there are a few people who remained with them. They have been handing over from one generation to another to date, especially in Northern Europe.

Descriptions and Alternate Meanings

Learning runes in their original runic language can be an uphill task for people who might be used to a different language like English. The starting point for learning should, therefore, be understanding the alternate meanings of runes in other languages, mainly English. Without a translation, runes become more mysterious, not forgetting that there are already many mysteries surrounding runes and their use. It is thus imperative for every learner to understand the various descriptions as well as meanings of various runic signs.

Illustrated in the table below are alternate meanings of the runic signs used in the 12th century. They are the sixteen runic signs that stemmed from the original 24 signs of the Elder

Furthark (explained later in chapter 2 of this book). Here we go:

Runic Name

Meaning

fè

wealth

úr

rain

thúrs

danger

ás

haven

reið

speed

kaún

disease

hágáll

hail

náúðr

need

isá

ice

ár

good harvest

sol

the sun

tyr

justice

bjárkán

spring

mádðr

humankind

logr

water

yr

endurance

The first step in learning runic languages should start with understanding the meanings of the various runes, mostly the sixteen, as they represent the recent signs that were finally picked after refining the old runic signs. After mastering these runic signs and their meanings, you can proceed to learn more about the special powers associated with each of these signs. You will also realize that there are different gods and goddesses associated with different runes. Remember that learning is only enjoyable when you understand what you are learning, and you can relate to a real-life situation.

When written in runic alphabets, runes tend to appear as strange things. But once the English meaning of the signs is given, it becomes easy to visualize what runic sign could be used for in real-life situations. As you will see later in this book, most runic activities, including rituals, practices, and exercises are things you can easily understand if you know their meanings. With the above table, you strange signs won't again strike you. Most importantly, you will be in a position to make translations from runic alphabets to English.

Gods and Goddesses Associated with Runes

Just as there are in many cultures in different parts of the world, there are gods and goddesses associated with runes. They are the drivers of the different forces responsible for different happenings or special powers. Here are the most common runic gods and goddesses:

Frey

Frey is associated with Ingwaz rune. He is the runic god of peace, plenty, happiness, sexual love, and abundance. He is also known as the protector of natural vegetation and fertility. Some writers and books call him the god of this world since most of the things he grants are seen as belonging to this world only and not the world of spirits.

Fry

Fry is associated with Perthro rune. She is the goddess of marriage, love, reconciliation, where there are a crisis, pregnancy, and childbirth as well. In a nutshell, she is the god of the family who takes care of different family affairs. Her desire to make sure that families are safe, protected, and have peace makes her a favorite goddess for families facing struggles and other problems that are a bit tough to solve.

Freyja

Freyja is associated with Gebo rune, and she is responsible for feminine beauty, sexual pleasure powers. Some books call her the lady as she is mostly concerned with showering ladies with beauty.

Baldur

Baldur is associated with Sowilo rune. He is the god responsible for light, joy, persuasion, and the power to reconcile warring parties. Since light is associated with the sun, rituals and gifts give to Baldur were mainly done on the day of the sun (Sunday).

Hands

Hands god is associated with Naudhiz, and he is the god of the moon. He was dedicated on Monday or the day of the moon. He is believed to preside over natural processes and timings just as different moon phases are used to make different timings or seasons. Hands can change cycles in favor of the needs of those who believe in him.

Heimdal

Heimdal is associated with Mannaz rune. He is the god who gives the ability to hear sounds, including the quiet ones that would go unheard. He is believed to have sacrificed his own ear to help his people get a unique power of hearing. Others also know him as the god who connects the earth and heaven.

Thor

Thor is associated with Thurisaz rune. He presides over deadly natural forces such as thunder and lightning. He uses these forces to keep the atmosphere free from chaos or any forms of distractions that tend to make it impure. Many believe that Thor uses a deadly hammer to keep things in order. The hammer is, however, not only for hitting wrongdoers, but it is also a sign of a hardworking god who helps men as they labor with their daily hassles.

Gefion

Gefion is associated with Jera and Fehu runes, and she is the goddess of virtue and women who are unmarried. She is also responsible for fertility and has the ability to shift shapes to match the different needs of those struggling with infertility. Her favorite colors are gold and green, which is a sign of fertility.

Sunna

Sunna is associated with Raidho, Ansuz, and Ehwaz runes. He is the god of powerful protection in times of need, inspiration, and general weather. Among all the gods and goddesses associated with different runes, Sunna is the most powerful and strongest of all. Just like Thor, he has the ability to wield a strong hammer that causes deadly lightning flashes upon the earth.

Many other runic gods and goddesses exist, but the ones discussed here are the most common ones who are often invoked for intervention in various human activities. Their special powers/forces and abilities to influence human activities positively is what makes them popular since the ancient times of Germanic people when runes were developed.

Chapter Two: Understanding Runic Alphabets

Traditionally known as futhark, the Runic Alphabet is believed to have stemmed from the Greek Alphabet. In fact, a couple of letters in the Runic Alphabet have a great similarity to those used in the ancient Greek version. However, that is not the only alphabet system that the Runic Alphabet bears resemblance with. It is also argued that it might have been developed from the ancient alphabets that were initially used in Italy. While little is known about the origin of Runic Alphabets, there is much that can be talked about when it comes to its development and change over time.

Types of Runic Alphabets

There are at least three different runic alphabets, namely Elder Futhark, Younger Futhark, and Medieval Futhark. While there are a couple of differences among these three alphabets, there are many similarities as well, bearing in mind that they are all Runic Alphabets. Their only major difference is the fact that they were developed at different times of history and have all had their own changes over time. To get a better understanding of each of these alphabets, here are the details:

Elder Futhark Runic Alphabet

Elder Futhark is the oldest Germanic runic alphabet. It was widely used in many parts of Europe until many years later when other alphabets came into existence. It is believed that all others that came after stemmed from the Elder Futhark. They emerged as a result of changes that occurred over time in the way the European people used their languages. Experts in the runic alphabet argue that the name Futhark was derived from the first six runes. Besides, there are 24 runic signs that represent different letters. The signs and the corresponding letters that the Futhark alphabet signs correspond to are illustrated here:

Regarding the origin of the signs used in the futhark alphabet, researchers seem not to have a consensus on it. In addition, the order of the letters used does not in any way narrow down to the usual letters of the alphabet (ABC...) since their development was independent of the already existing English letters of the alphabet. However, some scholars argue that the development of the elder futhark was inspired by the Etruscan writing as well as the Roman alphabet since those were the commonly used systems at the time.

A couple of Elder Futhark runic inscriptions have been found in many artifacts, some dating to as old as the 2nd century. The most common ones include runestones, weapons, and amulets, among many others. The inscriptions, of course, consist of twenty-four runes, but picked from the first six runes, namely F, U, P, A, R, K. Later during the Viking Age, the Elder Futhark runic alphabet was simplified to match the phonological changes that had occurred in the Germanic languages. More specifically, the number of runes was reduced by 8 to 16 to form the Younger Futhark.

Younger Futhark Runic Alphabet

History has it that towards the end of the 8th century, the spoken language had encountered a lot of changes, and there was a need to reform the runes. To illustrate the change, it is reported that the number of vowels had increased from the initial 5 to 9. Seeing the changes, one runemaster decided to change the runes by reducing them to 16. Further changes occurred in the 9th century, and eventually, in the 10th century, the changes were accepted in Scandinavia. The acceptance is what can be said to have given birth to the Younger Futhark alphabet.

The Younger Futhark Runic Alphabet has two variants, namely, the Long Branch, which is also known as the Danish variant, and the Short Twig runes, also known as the Swedish & Norwegian runes. The difference between these two variants is said to be in their use. For instance, the Long Branch runes were mainly used when making inscriptions on stones. On the other hand, the Short Twig runes were mainly used when writing official as well as confidential messages. The authenticity of these differences in use is, however, a subject of controversy with no clear explanation of their development.

Signs used in the Younger Futhark alphabet vary between the long-branch runes and the short twig runes. The variation is not, however, large between the two. In fact, some differences are just as a result of the simplification of runes of the other variant. More precisely, nine runes in the short twig runes are a simplification of those of the long-branch. The other remaining seven are just similar. Here are the illustrations:

Long Branch Runes

ᚡ

ᚢ

ᚦ

ᚯ

ᚱ

ᚴ

ᚼ

ᛏ

ᛁ

ᛐ

ᛂ

ᛏ
ᛒ
ᛉ
ᛚ
ᛑ

f
u
þ
ą
r
k
h
n
i
a
s
t
b
m

1

R

Short-Twig Runes

ᚤ

ᚿ

þ

ᚭ

ᚱ

ᚴ

ᚠ

ᚼ

ᛁ

ᚨ

ᛁ

ᛍ

ᚡ

ᛏ

ᛚ

ᛌ

f

u

þ

ą

r

k

h

n

i

a

s

t

b

m

l

R

A couple of years later, the younger Futhark runes saw another change. Signs that were previously not there were introduced. What exactly happened is that voiceless signs were introduced to denote their voiced counterparts. This essentially increased the number of runes from the original number that existed before the changed happened. The expansion of the existing runes is what gave birth to the next runic alphabet; the Medieval Futhark.

Medieval Futhark Runic Alphabet

The transition from the Younger Futhark to the medieval runic alphabet took place during the spread of Christianity in Scandinavia. It took place in the late 18th century, and it saw many changes occurring in the language system that was there previously. Although a lot happened at the time, runic masters argue that the change mainly involved the decoration of runes using Latin letters. Yes, it brought a new way of writing runes, but there were confusions, especially in the use of three letters, namely s, c, and z. In a nutshell, runes were Latinized to match the new Christian way of life that was rapidly spreading at the time.

While the wave of Christianity had a great impact on the use of runes, it didn't completely stop it from being used. Runes were, in fact, in common use side by side with the Latin system of the alphabet. In addition, a great interest in learning and use runes grew a lot in some areas such as Iceland after the 15th century. The tremendous growth is evident from the hundreds of Norwegian runic inscriptions that have been preserved in many archives to date. Many have been discovered over time, with the greatest ones being the 600 that were discovered in the 19th century in Bergen. This reinstates the fact that despite the reality that runes alphabets have been there for centuries, their usefulness is still great.

Today, there are still many people who use runes for different purposes. Discussions are ongoing on the best way to store and pass on the unbroken tradition that has stood the test of time to its current status. A lot has been written in books about runes and the continued growth of interest to learn and use them among many even in the 20th century points out the fact that they still have a special place and use as well in modern-day activities.

Misconceptions

You've probably have come across stories detailing the common misconceptions that exist about runes. They have been there since ancient times, and they are not about to vanish any time soon. Well, in all honesty, anything that seems difficult to understand or uses strange signs often attracts different interpretations, including misconceptions about it. Runes are not spared either. Those who have tried to learn but and left it on the way or couldn't just connect the dots to make meanings out of runes have many stories and myths about runes. If you come across some of those stories, you may no longer move on with your quest to learn runes and use them to improve your life. Misconceptions surrounding them are no doubt misleading, let alone the fact that they are discouraging. The most widespread misconceptions about include the claims that runes are no longer useful, they have no powers, are used by Satanists, can attract bad omen, and others. All these are just baseless claims spread by those who do not understand what runes really are and their role in humanity.

The truth is that runes are totally different from the messages that these statements send out, especially to unknowing rune novices. To set the record straight, runes are primarily used for communication. Like any language, it uses signs, and it has evolved over time. Besides, the use or runes in everyday activities simply is for the purpose of serving the specific use and not any hidden or specialized function that cannot be understood as is often said by agents of misconceptions. Also, when spells are carved into runes, the power comes from the spell and not the rune. Similarly, all other functions where runes are involved do not necessarily imply that anything unusual is from the runes. It could be a different force. For instance, there are gods and goddesses associated with runes. Anything good or bad associated with them belongs to the forces (gods and goddesses) and not the runes. Runes only help in connecting with these forces or powers that have an influence on human behavior.

Chapter Three: Spell Casting and Divining

Runes are said to have magical properties/powers that can be used in spell Casting and divining. Since time immemorial, runes have been used for many other activities apart from general communication. In this chapter, we delve into the use of runes for spell casting as well as divining. Although there have been many changes over the years, the fact remains that runic signs are still useful in many ways.

Meaning of Spell Casting

Spellcasting is a practice that has been there for many years. However, it has been misunderstood by many, especially those involved deeply in spiritual work. So what exactly is this practice all about? Well, it is simple. Just as we bring different letters to do works that finally combine to make meaning, so does spell casting work. It is about stringing things together to make something great that can enhance life. Spell casting is not, however, necessarily about changing things but rather supporting what our minds can do.

Contrary to the general beliefs, spell casting is about bringing oneself into proper alignment with the inner purpose. Therefore, people spell craft to change their own lives and not to influence the lives of those around them negatively. Just to illustrate this, we can use spell casting in our lives to attract something to our lives, strengthen our character, increase our self-confidence, and benefit ourselves. These are the ways in which spells are used, although the practice of spell casting varies from one place to another.

Apart from spell casting to improve our lives, spells can also be used in meditation to connect with other beings. Besides, other people use spell casting as a spiritual tool or as a divine power to deal with daily life challenges. Other than these, spells can be used in many other different ways. In addition, there are different levels of spell craft that can be used. With that said, spell casting remains an ancient practice that has stood the test of time to become an activity that is still applicable by many in different parts of the world.

Types of Spells

There are hundreds of different types of spells. In fact, there are spells of almost every activity or imaginable task. Human needs are unlimited and endless, as well. Therefore, there are spells for almost every need that a human mind would want to achieve. These spells also vary from one place to another and from one culture to another. And since there are many different cultures across the world, you can imagine how many types of spells exist in this world.

Protection spells, loves spells, abundance spells, wealth spells, trick spells, health spells, life spells, beauty spells, luck spells, weather spells, fantasy spells, and spirit connection spells are just a few types. As it is evident, these types of spells correspond to the different activities that people do on a daily basis. People do different things to achieve what they want, and spell casting is just one of the ways people try to enhance their living environment.

The Connection between Runes and Spell Casting

Runes are letters or individual elements which when they come together, make words that eventually make meanings. They can thus be used in spell casting, and in fact, many people continue to use them in different parts of the world. When runic signs are brought together, they make words and meanings that can be attached to these different words. People, therefore, use runes or rune casting to strive to achieve their daily needs. More specifically, runes are used to create a cause-effect and predict a likely outcome in one's life.

Runes act as excellent tools for spell casting. Just to illustrate this, runes may be used to create writings, curves, paintings, or castings with special meanings or powers. People can then use them according to their needs. This practice has been there for centuries, and even today, spell casting people still use them for different purposes. It is, however, worth noting that spell casting using runes or rune casting as some people call it is so diverse. As such, there is no single formula for doing it. It all depends on what one is interested in achieving at the end.

One popular way of using runes for spell casting is working with an individual or even a set of runes that is inscribed into an object so as to access the power associated with it. Powers associated with such individuals or sets of runes include healing power, luck in work, protection power, and many others. Runes, therefore, whether written or carved into an object, act as marks of protecting, healing, love, and other aspects of life already outlined. While sometimes these practices are condemned as witchcraft or magical works, they have remained popular for many years. To date, many people are learning the different ways of using runes for spell casting.

Indeed, runes spells are powerful and very useful to some people. On the other hand, some look at it as mysterious and things that belong to witches only. The reality, however, is that an everyday person can use runes for spell casting without necessarily doing it for witchcraft purposes. People who know what spell casting and understand its role use it to draw the things they need in life. It has worked for some, and many others are inspired to explore the power that exists in using runes for spell casting.

As a way of wrapping it up, if you are interested in testing the power of spell casting using runes, then there is a lot to do. First, understand what it is all about since there are so many misconceptions about it. The fact is that there are so many good things worth knowing about runes and spell casting. In fact, spell casting might just be what you need to change your life and find it easy to meet your daily needs. Many testimonies are there about the success of runes and spell casting. It is, therefore, a matter of how you perceive and use it.

Rune Casting Techniques

While the art of casting runes has changed over time, the fact remains that it is all about using runes to find meanings of hidden things and changing one's life as well. It relates things to find a possible cause-effect relationship and a likely outcome. Some of the common types of rune casting practices include the following:

Simple Rune Casting

As the name suggests, simple casting is easy to carry out. It does not require anything that is too special or out of the ordinary. To do it, simply take your bag of runes, stir it around to mix them up, and pick up a bunch. Throw them on a white cloth then keenly monitor how they land on the place you have thrown them to.

Some runes will face up, others down, and others upright. The directions they face have a meaning, and that's what you should interpret. You can formulate a question that relates to the puzzle that you are trying to unfold. If a rune faces a give direction, then it means a certain thing.

Spiritual Nine-Rune Cast

This is often done by people who want to obtain deeper insights about an event or situation that is facing them. Why nine runes? Well, in Norse Mythology, nine has a meaning as well as magical significance. To do it, pick nine runes randomly then hold them between your hands as you think about the problem you want to solve. Scatter them on a piece of cloth, on the table, or even on the floor.

How the results of nine rune casting are interpreted is subjective. Everyone has their own way of making meaning out of the results obtained. However, although there is variation, there a general rule regarding the nine-rune-cast is the runes lying at the center are the ones who carry the greatest meaning and relevance. You should, therefore, focus on interpreting them to help you answer your questions.

Ground Casting

Unlike the earlier types, ground casting is a bit unique in a couple of ways. First, it uses rune tines such as sticks and twigs on which symbols of runes are inscribed. Also, its interpretation is a bit simple. You just cast them on the ground then look at those that land upright. Their positions in relation to each other are also important in interpreting the outcome.

Regarding meanings, if runes cross each other upon landing on the ground, it means they are in opposition. If they are lying in a parallel position, they are related. Also, those that group far away from the others imply something too. You should, however, note that interpretation techniques applied here rely a lot on intuition. So you have to build your own techniques that suit your needs and situation.

Divining

In the simplest terms possible, divination can be explained as the act of trying to discover hidden knowledge or foretell what is likely to happen in the future. It is a practice that has been there for many centuries, and it continues to exist to date. The history of divination dates back to about 200bc when the people of Mesopotamia, Egypt, Canaan, and Anatolia, just to name a few, communicate with their deities through divination. This practice did not, however, end at the time. It has evolved over time, and many people in different parts of the world still practice it mostly for religious purposes.

Intuitive forms of divination are the most practices. It simply involves people using natural or human phenomena to reveal hidden things or tell the future. One common example to illustrate this is an analysis of stars, weather, birds' behavior, moon, and entrails to derive the meaning of various happenings. Some people also speak to the dead, cast lots, shoot arrows, or drop oil in water, all in an attempt to predict the future or interpret the hidden meaning of things that are happening presently.

Types of Divination Methods

Different methods of divination exist, and people use them depending on what they want to achieve at the end. Some methods are also common in some regions of the world, while others are promoted for religious purposes. Even more interesting is the fact that people choose what works best for them, leaving the other types. While there is no specific number regarding the types of divination, the most common types include the following:

Rune Stones

Runes stones, otherwise known as Norse runes, are also used in divination. They are carved into stone, and those who understand and use them argue that they are sacred and holy gifts that human beings can use. More specifically, they are often used to help in finding out what the future has or what events are likely to happen. One, however, has to understand the runic language, including runic alphabets, in order to make use of this divination method.

Numerology

Numerology in divination is simply the use of numbers to help reveal the hidden meanings of different mysteries or unforeseen future. The belief behind the use of numbers is the fact that they have magical and spiritual significance. In addition, some numbers of particular combinations of numbers are believed to be more powerful than others. They are thus used for divination practices.

Use of Pendulum

The use of a pendulum is the most common method of divination often used in different parts of the world. Its common use can be attributable to the fact that it helps solve simple puzzles just as everyday life choices. This method uses a weight that is attached to a chain or string and calibrated to help answer simple yes or no questions. Users argue that it is the easiest method of divination.

Automatic Writing

This method is one of the most popularly used ones when one wants to get messages from the spiritual world. It simply involves holding a pen and allowing the spirit to relay messages about any events or circumstances. One requirement here is that one should not apply any effort or think about what to write. Instead, they should allow the spirit to relay messages through automatic writing.

Unique Intuitive Ability

Although it is a rare one and is only used by a few people, intuitive ability is also another method of divination. In this method, one uses an extraordinary ability to know things without being told. It has been there for years, and it still exists to date. Like the other methods, it also helps uncover hidden things or tell what will happen in the future.

While there could be other methods of divination, these five are the most common ones. They are still used in many parts of the world among people of different cultures and religious beliefs. Some have, however, changed over time, and they are no longer done the way they used to be done in the past. For instance, some practices have been mixed with Christianity and hence transformed so that they are done in an acceptable Christian manner.

Runes of Divination

As already explained previously in this book, runes are said to have magical powers that can be used to meet human desires.

For instance, those who understand the runic language and its signs can cut runes to uncover a hidden thing or to cure a serious illness. Also, as part of the methods of divination rune, stones and signs can be used for different activities. Besides, there are different runic objects, including necklaces and other ornaments that are used as divinatory aids.

It is believed that Vikings (Inventors of runes) used runes for everyday activities, including divination. Although there is no clear evidence to support this, there are many runic activities and inscriptions that are connected with divination in many ways. For instance, runic readers believe that the future is not fixed. That is, one can change what will happen in the future by acting differently at present. Similarly, divination involves foretelling future events and changing behavior currently to avoid any future disasters. One can thus say that runes can be used for divination, especially when the intention is to explore the future and find out what it has for one.

One thing to remember is that although runic signs and stones can be used for divination, rune casting is not all about fortune telling as it is often made to appear like. It is simply a way of asking questions about the future or finding meanings of the present happenings that we would otherwise not understand without the use of runes. Most importantly, it is good to note that not all runic materials can be used for divination. The commonly used ones are stoned, pebbles, and inscriptions. Others, including bone, metal, and many other signs, serve other purposes. Either way, runes have a special role to play in everyday life and in the solution of human challenges, including the uncertainty of the future.

Take-Home Point

Rune casting, spell casting, and divination are not the same thing. Unlike the later, rune casting is not supernatural. Neither is it also superstitious. It is just about making use of your subconscious mind to connect things.

Chapter Four: The New World

The culture surrounding runes has been there for centuries, and it continues to find use even in modern-day society. To date, runic alphabets act as a symbolic representation of certain aspects of life. For this reason, those who understand it continue to apply it in many ways. However, there is another interesting thing that many people do not know. Almost everyone has used runes but most likely without their knowledge. In this chapter, we explore some of the technologies that make use of runes.

Bluetooth Technology

Let's face it! The Bluetooth technology has completely transformed communications and made work easier than it used to be. These days, we can easily connect to devices without having to use cables as they were in the past. Since its invention, billions of devices have created connections and shared data and information thanks to this amazing technology. Moreover, many other technologies have come as an improvement in technology. It has, therefore, acted as a base or reference technology for other inventors interested in adding features to what we are already enjoying.

Aside from the usefulness of Bluetooth technology, there is one interesting thing that many people do not know. Well, The

Bluetooth logo you see on your smartphone is a combination of two bind runes, namely Haglaz and Berkana. These runes are equivalent to letter "H" and "B," and they represent the initials of the name of King Harald Blåtand. He was the King of Denmark during the Viking age and tried to build connections across the borders of his country. Interestingly, almost everyone with a mobile device or smartphone has used Bluetooth to create connections and transfer files. However, not many people know the fact that the technology's name has a runic origin. Indeed, this is something interesting to explore if you like runes and would like to understand its applications even in modern-day society.

Why Bluetooth Is Named after Powerful King of Denmark and Norway

Bluetooth is named after Harald "Blatand," who was a king of Denmark and Norway. He is remembered for many things and especially his efforts beyond borders that sought to unify his people, including neighbors. While most of his subjects were pagans, King Harald embraced Christianity and worked tirelessly to spread the religion. He promoted the faith within his borders throughout his tenure. His main aim was to unify the people of Denmark and Norway. Perhaps Bluetooth is named after him because of the similarity between the work he did and what Bluetooth does these days. Well, the technology connects by going beyond the borders of a single device to help make communication easy.

According to some scholars, King Harald was got the name "Blatand," which means Bluetooth because he had a rare dental condition. He had a dead tooth that literally turned dark and bluish. That is what led him to get the name Bluetooth. How the name transferred to a telecommunications technology is, indeed, interesting. According to Jim Kardach, one of the founders of Swedish Telecommunications Company, Ericsson, the name Bluetooth was chosen for all the right reasons. The founders felt that Harald's ability to negotiate beyond borders and unite people was a great thing. They, therefore, saw it right to name their technology after the King since the intention of coming up with it was to 'unite" devices and make communication easy.

Since its invention and release, Bluetooth technology has, indeed, lived the life of the name it is named after. In fact, it had done much more than what the owner of the name did when he was alive. The technology has connected millions of smart devices worldwide and enabled communication. Most importantly, it has helped in the sharing of important files, documents, and anything worth sharing or transferring from one device to another. It is also great to note that other technologies have also borrowed from the features of

Bluetooth to help develop other similar technologies to help share information and resources easily.

In modern English, the Bluetooth logo is simply a combination of letters H and B. These two letters are the initials of Herald Bluetooth, the kind who died centuries, but his spirit of communicating across boundaries and among different groups live to date courtesy of powerful innovation. Letter H and B were, however, not written in Viking language the way they are currently written in English. That takes us to a very interesting question.

Can Modern English Be Translated to Runic Language?

The truth is that it is easier to translate the Runic language to English than to do the vice versa. Taking English names and translating to runes is a complicated procedure. It is an attempt to transcribe words whose sounds never existed in languages from which runic alphabets were developed. But that does not, however, mean that it cannot be done. With research and more studies on phonology, there might come a time when it will be possible to write whatever we want in English then have it translated into runes. If that happens, a lot will be achieved, and people will be able to create more runic exercises, and practices in their own language then have it put in runes for originality.

Away from translation, the fact that runic signs are being used in modern-day technologies, writings, and even in-wall decorations affirms the power that exists in runic language. Despite many changes that have occurred over time in runic alphabets, runes still exist to date, and more people are continuing to learn it. One distinguishing trait that could possibly explain the uniqueness of runic signs is the use of the same signs for voiced and voiceless consonants, a trait that is not existent in modern English.

Chapter Five: Witness Your Future

Runes are still used these days in many ways by those who understand them and what they are capable of doing. In this chapter, we explain how runes are used these days to make predictions about the future. In a nutshell, runes can help answer questions about the past, what is happening presently, and, most importantly, what the future has for one.

How Runes Can Be Used to Predict the Future

Runic readers argue that you can unlock your ability to connect with the sources of energy, healing & love and be able to tell what is likely to happen. This does not, however, imply anything to do with fortunetelling. On the contrary, what rune casting or the art of using runes to predict the future does is that it gathers a couple of variables and offers advice on what one can do in the event that something occurs. Simply put, runes give you hints of what is likely to happen but leaves you with the freedom to decide what to do now.

According to the assumptions of rune casting, the future is not fixed and that if you don't like the direction you are following presently, you can at any time divert. The implication of this assumption is that individuals have the power to make their own decisions and follow their own path. So if there is something you fear that it might happen in the future, you ought not to fear anymore as you have the power to change it. You can take a different route and see the future you desire unfolding before your eyes.

When Should You Resort to Rune Casting?

You can use runes in many situations depending on your circumstance and what you are really interested to know about the future. A good example is when you have limited information about a future event, or you want to act, but you have an incomplete picture of what is likely to happen. At such instances, consulting rune readers can help unearth the hidden future, so you can act accordingly.

When you can use runes, you are ideally asking a question or thinking about an issue. The idea here is to focus your conscious and unconscious minds to help you make a decision. Runes can thus be said to be useful when you are in a situation of indecision. It is, therefore, right to say that rune casting helps to bring out the decisions already made but not opened to you. Casting runes can thus help you get a better picture of what awaits you in the future and what to do if what awaits you is not what you have been anticipating.

Runes Used to Discover the Future

There are twenty-four different runes that you can use to discover your future. Each of them has a runic meaning as well as its implication for your life. Most importantly, they help answer whatever questions you have about the future. Therefore, when you cast them, the order in which they fall has a meaning in your life. They also determine your fate. Although there are renowned runic readers, anyone can cast runes and interpret if they have the knowledge of rune casting.

Here are the twenty-four runes you can use to discover your future and their corresponding meanings:

i. Fehu Rune: money, wealth, and material goods

ii. Uruz Rune: strength & manhood

iii. Thurisaz Rune: a new start

iv. Ansuz Rune: a signal or message

v. Radio Rune: travel

vi. Kaunaz Rune: fire

vii. Gibo Rune: blessing

viii. Wunjo Rune: happiness

ix. Hagalaz Rune: chaos

x. Nauthiz Rune: pain

xi. Isa Rune: frustration

xii. Jera Rune: Fertility and harvest

xiii. Eihwaz Rune: barriers/protection

xiv. Perth Rune: hidden things

xv. Algiz Rune: defense

xvi. Sowelu Rune: perfection

xvii. Tyr Rune: victory

xviii. Berkana Rune: rebirth or a fresh start

xix. Ehwaz Rune: overcoming obstacles

xx. Mannaz Rune: humanity

xxi. Leguz Rune: motherhood

xxii. Inguz Rune: beginning

xxiii. Degaz Rune: sunlight

xxiv. Othela Rune: possessions

There are different ways of rune casting to discover the future. If you want to give a try, then do not go for complicated procedures. Simply find a quiet environment that can allow your mind to focus on the issue or question at hand. Have the runes preferably the stones in a box before you as you meditate. After meditating, cast the runes onto a cloth, or a pouch then read those that are fallen the right side up. Check the bearing and try to interpret the meaning, as already explained. This is one of the commonly used methods, but there are also other alternatives.

Can Runes Help Predict Future Misfortunes?

Future runes are not only aimed at discovering good. As already hinted, there are used to tell what the future holds. Runes tell the future whether it is good or bad for you. There are, in fact, runic signs that are a sign of unfortunate occurrences on the part of humans. Those are the ones that can help predict misfortunes likely to happen in the future. There are many runes that can help predict any unfortunate happenings that are likely to be experienced in the future. That means that as you learn about runes, you should be a good student of both good as well as bad runes as they all have an influence on your living.

An example of rune that represents dark forces acting against human is the Thurisaz. The meaning of Thurisaz is ogre, and from ancient tales, ogres are hostile gods that threaten to destroy humans. If you cast your runes and what you see is Thurisaz, then that could mean that you are headed towards something that might not be good for you. For instance, it could mean that your timing is unfavorable if you were preparing to start a project.

Is It Possible To Carry Out Past and Future Cleaning Using Runes?

Although it is a little bit confusing and painstaking process, it is possible to carry out the cleaning of your future from any damage that you are likely to face. Similarly, it is possible to use runes to restore your energy or health that might have happened to you as a result of magical effects. Many people say that it is hard, but the truth is that if you are determined to rid you're your past and future of any unfortunate occurrences, then it is possible to do it.

Runes are highly versatile, and they can be used for different roles and purposes, including cleaning. You can, in fact, do whatever you want with runes provided you know what you are doing. Most importantly, you ought to aggressive in learning the different runes and how to apply them to make your life better. The learning process should actually be continuous with the goal of finding out new ways of using runes to make your life worth living.

For future cleaning, you'll need to be familiar with rues of constructing the future or shaping it up the way you want. You can, for instance, seek the help of Sunna, the most powerful rune with the ability to transform anything. If you combine the power of Sunna plus a couple of others that have powers for transforming human life, then you can be sure to change your future and make live knowing that there is no misfortune awaiting you.

Regarding damage suffered in the past that is likely to affect your future, you can use certain restorative runic combinations to overcome the effects. If left uncured, they can easily cause physical weakness, indifference, and spiritual emptiness. At the worst, people who are victims of such magical effects at some point even contemplate suicide or anything that can easily take away their lives.

Glyphs, staves, and bandages are a combination of runes that are often used to restore as well as cleanse. The process of carrying out these combinations is also not that tough. Simply choose that which will help you get back to the status or health condition. Once you pick a combination that best solves your problem, carry it on yourself as a picture for a period of nine days. These days are ideally the length of cleansing time. At the end of it, and if you had picked the best combination, it is possible to completely rid your life of any past magical effect that has been affecting you.

Note that cleaning or restoring alone is not enough if you are a victim of past misfortunes, and you even fear that you are likely to face a lot in the future. You need to go a step further and look for a way of protecting yourself. Without protection, you risk going back to the former self or state of trouble that you have been trying to emerge from. That again calls for learning about rune protection and how you can apply it to stay safe now and in the future.

Runes That Can Be Used For Personal Protection Going Into the Future

Turisaz, Teyvaz, Algiz, and Isa are the four runes that you can use to protect yourself from the impact of your feared enemies in the future. These four runes have powers to stop bad energy and forces that are threatening to destroy your future. Apart from using these runes to protect yourself, you can also use them to protect your loved ones, your home, and even your workplace if you fear that there are threats there too.

To enjoy the security of runes of protection, use a marker or a ballpoint pen to draw these runic signs on the wall, objects at home, or on your body. You should, however, note that with time, drawings tend to fade. More specifically, those on your body are likely to be washed as you bath each day. Therefore, a more permanent way to have the lasting symbols is to make special amulets of the images you want. Curving the sign or symbol on wood or stone would be the best way to put your protection in place permanently.

For clarity about the runes of protection, Teyvaz is the best rune to protect your business, money, and general financial situation. It has the ability to send back negative spells send to your business and also resist any circumstances that are likely to affect your finances negatively. For protection from jealous individuals, Isa is the best rune. For evil eyes, use Turisaz, and you will be safe. Apart from offering you the protection you need, these runes also attract good luck and bring happiness into your daily activities.

As a reminder, the magic properties, as well as the powerful protection of runes, depend on many factors, among them your understanding and use of them. You can only enjoy the benefits if you are a strict follower of instructions and if you have also perfected the art of connecting with runes perfectly. The most experienced users of runes also say that runes are not a quick solution to problems. You have to take the time to build their power by frequently using them until you master the best ways of harnessing their powers.

Chapter Six: Runic Exercises & Preparing Your Mind

Runic exercises support meditation as well as the psychological work of the body. While there are many ways to use runes to connect with the spiritual world, using the body can help is one of the ancient methods that have been proven to be highly effective. This chapter explores various aspects of runes exercises. It provides a guide to runic exercises, descriptions of different exercises (Both long and short), and ends by explaining the various benefits of runic exercises.

Guide to Runic Exercises

A guide is necessary when doing any activity. It provides directions to follow from the start to end. Most importantly, it prepares your mind by outlining what you should expect and be prepared to do. Before you get started with any runic practice or tasks to help you make your learning process simple, you ought to prepare your mind accordingly. Here is a precise yet detailed guide to runic exercises:

Prepare Yourself by Having Your Body Relaxed

Having your body relaxed is very vital when it comes to runic exercises. Also, a relaxed body is flexible, and the chances are that you are more likely to be effective in your exercises if your body is free. This means that you need to relax your muscles, mind, jaws, and eyes since these are the parts that play a vital role in learning.

To achieve a complete state of relaxation, you need first to solve your internal conflicts, put your mind in a state that is ready to learn, and, most importantly, achieve quietness. These are the essential things you need if you want to perform runic exercises easily and reap maximum benefits associated with them.

Control Your Breath

Runic exercises are about connecting with the spiritual world and inner self to help you deal with the challenges of everyday living. For this reason, proper breathing is very necessary for yourself before you embark on any runic exercises. Even when you start exercising, full conscious breathing is very vital.

It is, therefore, recommendable that you exercise the art of controlling breath way before you kick off the actual exercises. Practice complete exhalation and wait until the urge to breathe in comes naturally. Most importantly, at all times, allow your diaphragm, ribcage, and shoulders to move freely as you breathe.

Learn to Control Your Thoughts

It is important to control your thoughts before and, most importantly while exercising. If you let your mind roam around without concentrating on what you are doing, then achieving the results you want may be an uphill task. Controlling your thoughts here means making sure that what comes to your mind is all about what you are doing and how you can improve on it. In simple terms, let your mind get used to meditation mode. That way, you can easily concentrate on the task at hand and enjoy the full benefits of what you are doing.

Learn to Sing Sounds Properly

Some runic exercises include singing specific sounds. It is thus important to learn how to change pitch, vary sounds, and move the body. You need perfect this before you start whichever runic exercises you want to practice. Doing so ensures that all runic exercise procedures, including singing, won't challenge you once you start exercising.

If you feel that you might not be comfortable practicing in a group, then learn to do it alone. Privacy gives you the confidence you need to practice high and low pitches. While doing it, make sure to perfect the art of raising and lowering pitch. Most importantly, learn to feel the differences and various impacts of the different sounds that you'll be practicing. That's one way to enhance your practice sessions.

Purity Can Also Be a Necessary Condition

One last thing to remember is that some runic exercises need purity. You should thus learn to clean your body to wash off all impurities symbolically. In some instances and depending on the kind of exercises you'll be doing, it may be necessary to use certain oils or herbs to help you clean all impurities. Some runic rituals/exercises demand that you just be pure in body and, most importantly, in mind.

Following these guidelines will make your training or exercise sessions fruitful. Remember that you will not just be exercising, but you will be doing it to help you solve life problems and achieve your needs. You can only uncover the secrets of runes and enjoy their benefits if you prepare well and put your mind and body in the right shape.

Runic Exercise Descriptions

While there are many runic exercises, knowing some of them and understanding what it takes to do, one can be helpful as you develop your own exercises. Here, a few examples have been given to help you get a clear picture of an effective runic exercise that you can try. Here we go:

Exercise 1: A long Runic Visualization Exercise

Requirements

- Your runes
- Candles preferably purple ones
- Appropriate meditation music
- Incense
- Cinnamon
- Wormwood
- Dandelion
- Bay
- Jasmine
- Mugwort

Methods

1. Go to a private, quiet place. For ease of access and total privacy, your bedroom is the best place. So go there light your candles, burn the incense and play low meditation music to help you get to the right moods. Experts recommend non-intrusive classical music.

2. Sit, look around, and make sure you are comfortable in your sitting position. Make sure you have your bag of runes near you or simply on your laps. This stage should last for about twenty minutes to allow you to connect with your environment in readiness for the subsequent steps.

3. Relax your body, take deep breaths, and close your eyes, then try to banish all distractive thoughts not related to your exercise. At this stage, you do not need to have your bag or runes on the laps. You can put it aside to allow you to control your thoughts easily.

4. Open your eyes, take your bag and then, with the power of your hand, pick one using your sense of feeling without having to look at it. Hold it for about ten minutes, then put the bag aside once again.

5. Settle down, close your eyes, breathe slowly to relax your muscles, specifically those at the arms, legs, hands, and let it continue all the way to the brain. Finally, let the muscles in your face relax as well.

6. While seated, connect to the spiritual world by visualizing a journey to a sacred place with the intention of finding a solution to any problem that you are facing. It should take a bit longer, as is the climax, healing moment, or realization of your goal. Thirty minutes are okay.

You can imagine taking a walk to the river in a nice cool afternoon. It is generally warm, and a soft breeze from the river ruffles your hair as you walk towards or along the river bank. The air is filled with sweet songs of the birds singing to cheer the beautiful wildflowers as the wind swings them side-by-side.

While you cannot see or understand clearly where you are heading or what exactly you are going to do in the river, let the environment give you a fresh feel. Take a keen look at anything to help you concentrate and ask yourself a couple of rhetoric questions. Perhaps looking at a bird singing could be all you need to find a solution to that problem that has bothered you for long. Try to connect what you see with the happenings in your life.

Listen to your senses. What are you feeling, smelling, or hearing? Once you are satisfied and happy with the feeling, start the journey back. That possibly is an indication that you have undergone an inner change and experienced spiritual powers. Once you arrive back, open your eyes and take a deep breath.

7. After the small journey of meditation and experiencing a new environment away from your secluded bedroom, take the time to recover. You are most likely to feel tired, bearing in mind that any journey, whether a real one or an imagination makes you tired. A time to recover is thus essential before you complete your exercise.

8. Shut out the rest of the world, and get back to your room. Look up at the ceiling. What do you see? Is it the same thing you are used to seeing every day? You will most likely discover something you had not seen in the past. That's the essence of this exercise. To help you look at things differently and see life from a positive angle than you have always done.

That's one powerful runic exercise description that can completely change things in your life. As a reminder, you may not necessarily have to follow everything here religiously. You can add or subtract a few things to create your own unique program that matches your needs and the change you want to experience. Besides, not all runic exercises have to be too long as the one given here. There are short ones that are useful as well and can help you solve your problems effectively.

Simple Exercises

Exercise#1: Write a Poem for Every one of Your Favorite Runes

If you are a novice in runic exercises, then starting with the simple ones like writing poems can help you as you develop and learn the artfully. You can later get into the tough ones once you get started and fully understand the power of runic exercises.

Writing a poem for runes is a simple exercise since you do not need any special materials to have the job get done. All you need is bad of runes, a pen, and a paper to write on your favorite song or message to your runes.

Steps

1. Read about and understand all your runes

2. Find out the special powers associated with all your runes

3. Learn how to connect with the runes

4. Find out the historical contexts relating to all your runes

5. Write a nice sweet poem for each rune

Make sure that the poems you write help you understand and improve your relationship with every poem. Doing so will help you understand certain aspects of runes, such as the signs that you would otherwise not just understand by reading about them.

Exercise#2: Visualizing Runic Images

Image casting is also part of runic exercises, and one way to connect with the runes is to visualize their images. Sometimes, visualizing can help you see what you cannot see when your eyes are opened and looking at the runes.

Steps

1. Pick a rune and visualize its image forming right in front of your eyes

2. Chant its name as you visualize the image

3. Look at the rune and sing what you see

4. Continue singing for about 15 minutes each time including the name of the rune as you sing

5. Ground yourself and write whatever you saw and felt while visualizing the rune

Please beware that you can do this for every rune for as long as you want. Each time, try to see what you have not seen before in the rune, you are visualizing. You can also do it a couple of times a day, as it is a process that has no end. It is the best thing to do if you want to master rune casting. Therefore, take the time and practice it well until you master it well.

NOTE: As you perform these or other runic exercises of your choice, always try to ensure that nothing disrupts the flow of energy in your body. That's why your choice of a private or secluded room is very vital. It determines how you will go about the process and the results, as well. Usually, many people prefer a quiet place in the garden or simply in the bedroom, as was illustrated in the first exercise. Such places allow you to concentrate and increase your overall energy in the body, which you need to complete an exercise successfully.

Benefits of Runic Exercises

Persons of all ages and from different cultures use runic exercises for many reasons. Despite the great variation in the types of exercises performed, the benefits enjoyed cut across and in fact, are similar. Some do the exercises to obtain their daily needs. Others do it since they are interested and have been doing for years. Also, others are much into the benefits of mental exercise and fitness associated with runes. Irrespective of the reason for doing the exercises, the benefits do not discriminate against anyone. Here are some of the assured benefits of regular doing of runic exercises:

Improved Quality of Life

Invoking rune spells or signs associated with happiness such as WUNJO, ALGIZ, and BERKANO can help improve one's quality of life. Different people invoke different runic forces and powers. The good thing about runes is that you don't have to stick to a particular method to enjoy its benefits. You can have your own runic activities that match your specific needs. The best way is to focus on those that will help you overcome your weaknesses and improve your overall quality of life. It might take time to master runes and what it is capable of doing, but the journey is worth it.

Improved Mental Fitness

As illustrated in the example exercises given, runes engage the mind taking it through simple as well as tough workouts through imagination as well as visualization. It is, therefore, almost obvious that when runic exercises become part and parcel of daily routine, the assured benefit is mental fitness. Some people, in fact, use runes to sharpen their minds and put them in better fitness levels. If you are experiencing any forms of weaknesses in the mind and you wish to overcome, then exercising runic activities can help solve the problem.

Achievement of Short and Long-term Plans

Everyone has ambitions and things they wish to achieve in the short run, as well as after a couple of months or even years. Learning runic signs and applying them appropriately can help one remain on the right track that leads them to achieve what they have planned for themselves. Some plans tend to be hard, and achieving them requires extra inspiration and dedication. With the help of runic exercises and other practices, such plans can be made simple and realistic. How it works is that runic exercises put your mind in the state of achievement, and once the mind wins it, you already have it.

Discovery of Secrets

Through runic divination, one can uncover hidden secrets and even find out what the future holds. How is this possible? There are many ways to do it. It can go through rune tossing, arranging them in certain styles, and putting together a couple of them to make a certain unique pattern. Meanings can then be attached to them to help discover secrets. For many years, people have been using this method to solve simple yes/no puzzles and even interpret complex secret situations. Although there are no specific procedures of making the discovery, different people apply the methods they understand to make meanings out of otherwise unknown events of happenings.

A Chance to Connect with Nature

Runic meditations are not just a way of understanding runes, but they also help in doing what one would not do without runes. For instance, the art of connecting with nature is not a usual thing but a special process best done with runes. Since ancient times, runes have played a very vital role in communicating with nature and understanding what it needs or what it can give to those who know its power.

Chapter Seven: Rituals to Accompany the Study

Learning runes cannot be complete without exploring a couple of rituals that accompany different runic activities. In this chapter, we delve into the topic of rituals in the context of runes. Although different people create their own runic rituals depending on what they are using runes for, there are common ones worth knowing. With that said, here we go:

Why Rituals Accompany the Study of Runes

When learning anything new, people often have different ways of making their learning process easy and enjoyable. In schools, for instance, some concepts are taught with the aid of experiments. The reason for having such practical activities is to make it easy to understand what's happening and also make it easy for learners to remember. Similarly, in the learning of runes, rituals act as 'experiments' that make the process simple and enjoyable as well. They add the spices to the process hence giving the learner a reason to go further and not just get the basics.

Rituals are not, however, meant to replace the real learning process as some people tend to argue. Rather, it is meant to supplement it. Besides, runic rituals are not static. They change over time, and you can even have your own rituals to make your learning process unique. For this reason, there are ancient runic rituals as well as those of the 21st century. If you want to understand runes better, create your own runic rituals. But remember that if you want to create perfect ones, you must first learn from the existing runic rituals. It, therefore, makes sense to understand a couple of runic rituals that have been in use since the long-gone days when runic alphabets came into being.

Common Runes and Their Corresponding Rituals

While they were initially used as a form of language in Germanic cultures in Northern Europe, runes are also powerful spiritual tools. They have been and are continuing to be used for religious purposes, divination, and magic, as well. Runes are, however, extremely versatile as they vary from one place to another and from one culture to another as well.

Here are five common runes and rituals to accompany them:

#1: BERKANO

The BERKANO rune is all about new beginnings and manifestations in one's life. It helps in making it easy for you to bring to life whatever new thing you want. It could be a new home, project, job, business, or even welcoming a new child. Anything that you are working hard to make it a reality, Berkano can help you bring it to reality.

BERKANO Ritual

Connecting with the power of Berkano is not difficult, and anyone can easily learn it. To perform this ritual, you need a stone, paint, or anything that can help you make a permanent mark. Besides, this ritual is often performed once the full moon is sighted. Once are these conditions are met, then you can connect. Simply visualize the new thing you want in your life, and as you think about it, make a painting or drawing of it on the stone. Place it in a place you'll be seeing as often as possible.

#2: WUNJO

Wunjo is all about happiness and overcoming any life hassles that bring sadness, anxiety, and other feelings that take away joy and happiness. Let's face it! Almost everyone undergoes different life happenings that bring sadness. It happens, and it is not a surprise. If you feel that you are overwhelmed, then Wunjo is all you need to be happy. It will grant you the happiness you need, even when things are tough on your side.

Wunjo Ritual

The Wunjo ritual is performed on the night of the first appearance of the full moon. Some people, however, tend to overlook this and perform it anytime. To perform this ritual, you need to make a sacred place or an altar, as is usually called in religious language. Put all things that make you happy on that altar. Make sure to pick those that make you the happiest when you see them. Look at your altar every day, and you'll always be happy.

#3: ALGIZ

If protection is all you need, then ALGIZ rune can completely change your life and provide a sense of protection you need in life. Algiz is not only a sign of protection, but it also helps you connect to your higher self and feel deeper inside you that you are safe. Many people often use this rune at times of crises, such as feeling scared and in need of protection in daily activities.

ALGIZ Ritual

Unlike other rituals that have to be strictly performed during specific moon phases, you can perform the ALGIZ ritual during any phase of the moon, although there are arguments that the dark phase is the best. To perform this ritual, you need three sticks, one long stick, and two shorter ones. Place the shorter ones at the center of the long one to make a v shape that looks like the Algiz symbol. Hang it on the wall or put it on your altar. It will provide the security you need, and you'll feel safe.

#4: TIWAZ

Also called the warrior rune, Tiwaz is known for its ability to strengthen people who are going through different difficulties of life. Whether you have a legal battle, facing indecision, have disagreements, or advocating for justice, Tiwaz might just be the rune you need to change things in your life. It is a powerful rune known for providing great strength.

TIWAZ Ritual

The Tiwaz Ritual is often performed during the first quarter moon. To do it, you simply need three things, namely a candle, a lighter, and a toothpick. You may, however, have to get many candles as you will need one for each problem you have. For instance, you may need a candle for your legal battles, disagreements, and other issues. Light the candles and sit with them until it is over, then you can extinguish it. You can, however, put it off when you finally win the legal battle you had, find justice, resolve a disagreement, or any other problem.

#5: FEHU Rune

In all honesty, we all love abundance, and in fact, we always strive to make sure that we have it as much as possible. Besides, our daily struggles are mainly to help us make ends meet, get daily bread, and enjoy many other blessings. However, getting all this is often not an easy job. Fehu helps during struggles and makes us enjoy abundance amidst great adversities and daily struggles.

FEHU Ritual

To perform the FEHU Ritual, you need a green candle, a lighter and a needle, toothpick, or anything that can help you carve the Fehu symbol on the candle. Carve the symbol while thinking of you enjoying blessings, wealth, and being showered with goodies. Once you are through carving, light the candle and look at it quietly to enjoy the power of Fehu and is the ability to bring abundance.

There are many other runic rituals for almost all the challenges we face. As already hinted earlier in this chapter, the one good thing about runic rituals is the fact that you can come up with your own rituals depending on your needs. But as a reminder, when you decide to create one for your needs, remember three things. It must be simple, done consistently until you overcome the challenge and it must help you overcome the problems you have at any given time, Runic rituals work, and there are many testimonies about the power of these simple yet effective runic activities.

Tips on Taking up Ritual Runes

Runic rituals can be performed individually or as a group. Whichever route you take, the results depend on many factors key among them being your own belief on the power of runes. If you don't believe it, then there may be no need to try all these experiments and practices. However, if after learning, you finally understand and see the power that exists in runes, then taking them up or putting in practice can change your life completely.

If you want to try runic rituals for your very first time, you need to have a small guide to act as your traffic lights. Proceeding without anything to warn or caution you on how to go about different activities can be a challenge. Fortunately, runic rituals are not very complicated as they are made to appear sometimes by those who have a negative view of it. Here are simple guidelines on performing runic rituals:

Outline Your Reasons For

You definitely have reasons that are propelling you to consider resorting to runic rituals. It is, therefore, good to put them down before you even start thinking of which runic rituals you'll perform. Writing them down and checking often will drive you to learn and perform rituals to accompany your study of runic language and signs.

Decide the Time and How You'll Perform Your Rituals

Different rituals are suited to different times. Before you start using runic rituals to help you meet the needs of your life, it is important to understand the best times to use them. Most importantly, make sure you know how to perform them and connect to their power.

Find Out If You Have All Materials of Requirements

Runic rituals can only be performed successfully if you have all the necessary materials or requirements for the rituals you are considering. If you do not have, then find a way of getting them before you start the experiments

Decide How You Will Go About Your Runic Ritual Sessions

Will you perform one by one or combine a couple of rituals at once? How you organize your rituals has an impact on the possible outcome that you will experience. It is always good to do them one by one, so you give full attention and harness full energy from each. If you combine many, the chances are that you might get mixed up and fail to concentrate fully. Remember that runic rituals are spiritual tools that work depending on the power of your imagination.

Take Up the Rituals

Finally, after learning and making sure that everything you need to perform runic rituals is available, the next big challenge is to do the actual job. As illustrated in the five examples of some common runic rituals, performing them may not be complex. However, the environment, and how you perform them is what determines the kind of results you will get at the end.

In some instances, it may be good to perform some runic rituals as a group rather than working alone as an individual. In such instances, you need to get like-minded individuals, preferably those facing the same challenges you have, so you work together. You should also note that group rituals might be a bit different from those that you can perform alone. That, therefore, calls for more research and learning about the difference between individual runic rituals versus those that can be done in groups.

In a nutshell, learning runes should not just be about reading about how they work and the situations they can help. It is good to go another extra mile to practice a few as you advance to the next higher stages. Runic rituals are highly versatile and tend to vary depending on what they are used for by those who understand them. Those who have taken the time to learn about them and their power have moving stories. If you want to give them a try, you need to understand them well and get the truth about the many misconceptions about them. You might end up realizing that all you needed to turn around your life was the power of runes and runic rituals.

Chapter Eight: Facts about the Blank Rune and Whether You Should Read It

One interesting question that rune enthusiasts often ask is what's up about the blank rune, and can anyone use it? Well, indeed, there is a lot to learn about this kind of rune, especially for beginners who would like to have a complete understanding of the runes before using them. It is also quite interesting to note that some rune users argue that the blank rune was not there in the past, and it was just introduced recently. Is it true? Did it ever exist in the past? What exactly does it mean? Well, these are the questions that this chapter will answer. If you ever had questions about this rune, you now have the best and most comprehensive answers.

Who Came Up With the Blank Rune?

A new age author by the name Ralph Blum is believed to be the inventor of the blank rune. Until the year 1982, he was famous for being a novelist of Jewish origin. His critics argue that until then, Blum had no knowledge of runes, Norse culture, history, or mythology. His decision to shift his attention to the new area might have been influenced by the growing demand for knowledge and insights about runes. In his admission, he agrees that, indeed, the new-age goldmine is what beckoned him to the art of reading runes and writing about it. He, therefore, enjoyed the new waters to the point of inventing something that no one had ever thought would exist in the world of runes.

Ralph Blum argues that he happened to get a set of runes from England that contained a 25th blank tile, probably a bonus rune or a spare just in case one of the 24 is not that good. Since he didn't know anything about the blank 25th rune, he took it and attached a new meaning to it. He referred to it as a blank, mysterious rune with a deep mystical meaning. After examining it for a while, he went ahead to write a book called The Book of Runes that explored all the runes in his set, including the 25th mysterious one that had never appeared in any book before or historical facts about runes as well as their origins.

Readers of Blum's book and especially the critics argue that the inclusion of the 25th tile is the biggest fraud ever invented in the history of runes. They further argue that even the 24 others, as explained in his book, had the wrong explanations too. However, that did not deter Ralph Blum from continuing to deepen his mind and pen in the world of runes. He went ahead to promote his book and especially the new invention; 25th tile. His view is that there was something great worth knowing about it, especially for purposes of blending it with culture.

Since the invention, there have been many other developments as well as controversies regarding the existence of the blank rune and its role. For those who are seriously interested in the old number of runes and meanings, the 25th is nothing. On the other hand, for the advocates of the new age runic knowledge, this is something great to explore. As a reader, you can choose whether you should stick to the old number or embrace the new age meanings. The fact, however, is that the blank rune was never in the initial 24 runes of Odin, the God of true and wise runic knowledge.

What Exactly is the Blank Rune?

Also called Odin's rune or the Wyrd rune, the blank rune is a new age thing that came into the limelight around the 1980s when it was marketed by some rune enthusiasts as an alternative form or a divination method that is only applicable in specific situations. It is regarded as a new thing or an introduction since there is no historical as well as archaeological evidence that the blank rune was ever among the original 24 runes of god Odin.

So what exactly is the blank rune if there is no historical evidence that it existed in the past? Well, the blank rune is the zero, or silence that is void of infinite possibility. Some writers or books describe it as the breath before a speech or the space between words. Besides, it is an element of air whose Tarot equivalent is the fool. This fact about the blank rune is the reason behind the debate on whether the blank rune is a good or bad omen. It is the reason behind the many talks and the debate about its use.

Essentially, the blank rune opens up a new chapter or space for discussion to a student or any learner of runes to put their wisdom into the questions often raised about runes. Those who have delved into this topic argue that the blank rune represents a situation of not knowing what is happening. Before the runemaster (god Odin) received the 24 runes, he was in a state of bot known as simply a state of ignorance. It, therefore, invites everyone to ponder on how it feels to be in the state of not knowing or awaiting the intervention of the giver of power and knowledge to provide the missing information.

Should You Use the Blank Rune for Divination?

Well, there is no straight answer to this question that continues to puzzle many and especially those still learning about runes. Some object it for technical reasons, and some are opposed to the blank rune because of their conservative nature. As a reader, you can, therefore, decide whether or not you are going to include it when casting or drawing your runes.

Some readers argue that including a blank rune in your set opens up a new page of complications, especially in interpretations. They say that it amounts to reading the air, meaning that there is nothing serious or tangible worth interpreting. On the other hand, some have used it, and they believe that including it opens up your mind for a conversation.

Rune teachers do also have varied opinions on whether one should include or exclude the blank rune. However, there seems to be a consensus in one thing regarding the use of this rune. They agree that things evolve with time, and as a result, having the 25th rune can as well be an indication that things have changed since Odin, the runemaster, introduced the 24 runes. Many teachers, therefore, advise their students to use intuition when deciding whether or not to include the 25th rune in their set. It is interesting to note that some even argue that it should be included since runes may not have been finished by the time Odin received them. In the same measure, there are those teachers that say that it is not right to have something that does not stand for anything.

Well, from the analyses of those who care for and those against it, one can conclude that there is no consensus on this. It is, thus, a matter of personal preference. You can have it, but whether to use it or not is purely a matter of personal choice.

For runic studies, there is no doubt that learning about the blank rune is very vital. Most importantly, knowing it helps you get facts, so when you decide to give it a try, you know exactly what you are using and where it came from since it was not in the original 24 runes given to Odin.

Assuming You Use, What Does It Mean When a Blank Rune Appears In Your Reading?

If you finally decide to have a set of 25 instead of 24 and you get the blank one a part of those you should read and interpret, what does it mean to have it? Well, this is where the knowledge of how to interpret the blank rune comes in. It has a meaning for your divination, and it might help you get the true picture of the situation that you are trying to solve. It has an implication though there is no uniform meaning of it.

Different rune teachers and users attach different meanings to the blank rune. But generally, what many of them tend to suggest is that having a blank rune suggests that there are complications in your divination practices. It can be a suggestion that your formulation of the question is ill-informed, or it is simply not right. Besides, it might be a call for you to meditate and wait before you can finally uncover the problem that you are facing.

To help you understand more about the blank rune, here are some of the responses that some authors or books have to say:

According to Farnell (2006), in his book about runes, a blank rune indicates that some sort of change is about to take place, but there is no clarity on whether the change is positive or negative. You may, therefore, have to do further reading to understand what exactly awaits you or what kind of change is going to happen to you sooner or later.

Peschel (1989) asserts that when a blank rune appears, it means that something you did not expect is going to come your way. However, whether it is good or a bad thing depends on your past behavior. If you did good things in the past and your behavior warrants it, then you should expect good, and the vice versa is also true.

Blum (1983), the inventor of the blank rune, also has his interpretation of this interesting rune. He argues that the appearance of this rune in a cast or a drawing can portend death. However, he does not simply mean that you are going to die if you cast or draw your runes, and a blank one becomes part of those that you should read. Death, in his explanation, is relative to any part of your life. It could mean the end of a relationship, business, or any other thing that has been alive and happening in your life.

According to Holmes (2013), the appearance of a blank rune indicates that there is some good progress in one's spiritual development. It also implies that one's knowledge is greater and even far much stronger than it was ever imagined. It is this a reminder that life is not that bad as one tends to imagine or think about, especially in times of hardships or some sort of desperation.

Vital Things to Remember About the Blank Rune

Having explored details about the blank rune, how it came to being, and whether or not you should use it, there are vital things to remember about it. Knowing them can help you, especially when you are faced with a situation where you have to decide whether or not you should include the additional blank rune in your set. You should note that as already, the decision on whether or not you should add it depends on what you intend to achieve. Precisely, there is no restriction or permission on whether or not you should use it.

Additionally, the other thing worth remembering is that the blank rune was not originally among the twenty-four that were given to Odin. It is something that came up much later in the 1980s from Ralph Blum. However, his invention was not intentional but rather something that arose from the runes he received from England that included an extra blank one. Instead of using it as a spare, he decided to give it a meaning, and it has since been used and included in many other recent publications about runes.

It is also worth noting that there are several other authors apart from Ralph Blum, who have also looked at the aspect of the blank rune and given it a meaning. As already shown on what it means to have blank runes, there are lots of things that can be associated with the rune. If you decide to use it, you need to understand the different views that some authors and runic teachers have about it. You might also have to read and interpret it if you cast or spread leads you to it or brings it up as one of your runes to interpret. Finally, there is no consensus on whether it is good or bad to include the blank rune in your set.

Chapter Nine: Runic Spreads

Runes are often arranged in different patterns for divinatory purposes. The patterns they form when cast or arranged are the "Runic Spreads." These spreads vary a lot, and they can range from as few as only two runes put in a sequence to as large as a full 24 runic layout pattern. In a spread, whether large or small, the most important thing is the sequence. It determines not only the position but the significance as well.

Different people make use of different spreads depending on their circumstances and the kind of information that they would like to obtain. More specifically, some people have one or a few chosen spreads, while others make use of different spreads. It is also interesting to note that spreads change from time to time, and they also vary from one place to another. If you love using runes to get information or knowledge of the unknown, you can also invent your unique spread that matches your needs. But to get a picture of what others usually do, you might have to learn and master some common spreads.

Common Runic Spreads

Single Spread

The single runic spread is the easiest and the simplest of all. It is often done when the situation at hand is not complex or when one needs a quick insight into what drives a particular situation. You can also apply when you want to get the most concise summary of a situation. In all these situations, a single rune spread provides an overview of what lies ahead and any guidance that one needs to tackle the problem at hand.

The procedure for drawing a single rune is also simple and straightforward. Hold your bag or runes then think about the situation that you are facing. For instance, you can say that you would wish the rune to give you a picture of the day ahead, comment upon an endeavor, or a problem. Once you clearly state what you expect to achieve after spreading, pick a rune then meditate while holding it. You can then look up its meaning, and you'll be done. Indeed, it is without any doubt the quickest, simplest, and most importantly, effective.

Three Spread

If you want to place an issue in its content and get an overall picture of it, then the three runic spread is all you need. It uncovers vital details about an event and what awaits you going forward. More specifically, it shows what led to an event, the issue itself that you are currently facing, and any possible outcomes that you should anticipate. In a nutshell, a three runic spread shows you three important things:

- Your past and circumstances that led to it

- Your present situation

- Your future, so you prepare

You need three runes to do this spread, but you will draw them one by one, each of them representing the three highlighted scenarios. Think about an issue, and when it is clear on your mind, draw your first rune. Have a flashback of the events that led to it while focusing on the drawn rune. Draw the second one while focusing on your current situation. Finally, draw the last one while focusing on what is likely to happen in the future. One thing you need to remember is that deep focus is very vital at all these stages.

Fork Spread

This kind of spread is often preferred by people who want to understand the dynamics of a given situation. It uses three runes that represent three different aspects of an important decision that is about to be made. If you are at a critical point where you are expected to make a decision, then this can be the runic spread to consider.

Drawing the three runes for fork spread is also a simple exercise. Each of the three runes you draw explains something about your decision. The left rune stands for the best possible outcome. On the other hand, the right one represents the second-best possible outcome, and lastly, the third one stands for the underlying critical factor that determines the outcome of your situation.

Diamond Spread

When something happens or a situation changes to something that was not anticipated, people believe that forces are acting or influencing it. However, understanding those forces, especially when one is looking for a solution, can be a challenge. Fortunately, there are runic spreads that can help reveal the forces acting on a given situation at hand. Such runes are, therefore, the best when you want to understand a hidden conflict.

Diamond rune spread is one type that can help reveal the hidden or dynamic forces acting on a given situation. You can thus opt to use this spread if there is a serious hidden conflict that is affecting you, and there is a need to reveal it. It is a four-runic spread with each rune representing a given aspect of a situation at hand. The four runes and what they represent in a given situation are given as:

Bottom rune: the basis of the issue of the problem

Left rune: one of the forces behind a given conflicting situation

Right rune: the other force that is acting on the situation you are facing

Top rune: what you can finally achieve by taking a given route

One thing that makes this kind of spread popular among many people is the fact that it can be used in a variety of situations. It doesn't matter the situation or conflict that you are facing. Provided you know how to draw it, you can, without any hassle, use it and get to understand the forces acting and what your remedial actions are likely to yield.

Norn Spread

The Norn spread is used when one wants to plot elements, including those of the past, the current ones, and even those expected in the future. It essentially helps in getting an understanding of the evolution of a situation over time. To perform this spread, you need three runes, namely, the left, right, and middle runes. Here are the three crucial elements that these three runes represent:

- Left: an important element of the past

- Middle: a deciding element of the present time

- Right: a critical element of the future

Relationship Spread

People relate, and there are usually many questions and issues involved in relationships. The relationship spread, therefore, helps people who want to understand the purpose of the relationship as well as what to expect going forward. More specifically, it explains the role of each partner and, most importantly, the direction that the relationship is likely to take it the future.

The relationship spread uses three runes, each representing an important aspect of the relationship. The first rune represents the attitude towards the relationship that the person drawing the rune has as well as their energy. The second rune represents the attitude and energy of the partner towards the relationship. Lastly, the third rune shows the reason the partners are in the relationship.

Elemental Spread

The elemental spread uses four runes with each rune representing a certain quality. The runes are namely, the top (Earth), the right, the bottom, and the left rune. In this arrangement, the top rune, which is also called the Earth, represents lessons that one can learn on the physical plane. The right rune represents lessons that are to be learned on the mental plane or those that one is thinking about with regards to the situation at hand. The bottom rune, which is sometimes known as the fire, represents lessons that one can learn from the spiritual realm. Finally, the left rune; water stands for emotional lessons.

Celestial Spread

Unlike all other spreads, the celestial spread takes the longest time and uses more runes. Ideally, it takes a whole year, and one needs a total of thirteen runes to do this kind of spread. Those who draw this spread often use it to get a glimpse of the kind of influence that the year has on their life. The thirteen runes are arranged in a diamond shape with the first one being the right rune to the last one, which is rune twelve.

It is, however, worth noting that since the celestial rune does not have to start in January since it is a whole year practice. It can start at any month, and the first or the right rune represents the month that you are in. If you, thus, start in June or say August, all you need to do is to follow the diamond shape every month until the twelfth rune. Finally, when you are done, the last one, which is the thirteenth, will give you the influence that the year had on your life or the situations you had over time.

Celtic-Cross Spread

If you are well versed in star crosses or the patterns they form, then understanding the Celtic cross spread is pretty simple for you. This kind of spread is applicable in situations where you want to gain a complete view of the situation that is affecting your life. You can use it to plot the arc of your life, so you get a complete view of what is happening and where you are likely to be headed to in the future.

Celtic cross is a ten-rune spread. When drawn, they all form a right, left, and center pattern that represents various times. All runes to the left side represent the past with the furthest giving details of the distant past. On the other hand, all runes to the right represent all future times with the furthest giving details to the distant future. The rune at the center represents the current situation.

Odin's Spread

Named after the Norse god, Odin, this is a five rune spread that helps in understanding the past, present, and future. Two left runes; the far left and left represent distant past and recent past, respectively. Two right runes; far-right and right represent distant future and near future, respectively. Finally, the one remaining rune at the center or top represents the present time.

It is good to note that unlike the other rune spreads that are also used to get information about the past, present, and future, Odin's spread is a bit detailed. Precisely, it looks at these vital things deeply as it gives you an option to understand distant times. It is, therefore, the best when you want to get a complete understanding of a given situation with regards to times, especially the distant past, as well as the future.

Medicine Wheel Spread

If you ever find yourself in a situation where you do not know exactly which path you should follow, the medicine wheel spread can help you. It gives guidance on a specific issue that the person drawing or casting has at hand. Many times, this spread is utilized when there is a need to understand which path is likely to lead to the desired destination.

To draw the medicine wheel spread, you need to have five runes, namely the left, right, bottom, top, and center. The bottom rune provides details about the flow of energies or the future specifically. The top deals with or shows you the challenge at hand. The left rune uncovers the source of the problem. On the other hand, the right rune represents the current situation. Finally, the fifth rune stands for the power that you can call upon to intervene and fix the situation that you could be facing.

Other runic spreads exist, and some people even come up with their spreads that reflect their different situations. Provided you understand the art of drawing runes, there is nothing that can prevent you from coming up with your own unique spread that is specific to the situation that you are facing at hand. It is, however, recommended that when beginning,, you start with those commonly used and simple ones before progressing to the complicated types.

Chapter Ten: Hidden Runic Roots

While the history of runes reveals much information about how runes came to use, there are other interesting hidden roots that every reader should know. For instance, the Shamans in Scandinavia used runes as their protective symbols. They carved them into stones, woods, and bone, and there were lots of mysterious stuff about runes. Other than that, there are lots of other things that a student or anyone learning about runes should explore. In this chapter, we take a look at a couple of those hidden runes.

The Hidden Process of How Odin Got the Runes

Odin consistently sought new knowledge, and the process that he used to gain the knowledge of runes is quite interesting, yet it is not fully disclosed. Other than being the inventor of runes and many other things related to it, he is also known as the god of magic or wisdom. Indeed, his wisdom is what made it possible for him to attain knowledge that would otherwise be impossible in human ways. To gain absolute knowledge, Odin had to renounce an eye. That's, in fact, how he managed to drink from the rarely known spring of wisdom that not everyone makes to reach or even know where it is found.

To surrender himself to the world of wisdom and drink from what others could not, Odin had to hurt himself even after removing his eye seriously. He pierced himself using a spear and hang down from a tree for two days. All these activities happened far away in a cold place where no one could see what he was doing. When he was almost dying, 18 magical runes were revealed to him, and they were rapidly spread throughout the world. They were later increased to 24 after he successfully managed to cheat death narrowly. He had successfully conquered death and managed to drink from the spring of wisdom that no one else had eve tested.

Since their introduction and spreading across the land by the powerful god who conquered death, runes have kept their magical properties over the years. Most importantly, they have been successfully used for many different purposes. For instance, they have been used over the years for protection, flight, and even contacting death. Besides, they have been used as a way of making contact with other plains of existence through divination. To date, runes still play a very vital role in the daily lives of many people, mainly runic enthusiasts.

Hidden Connection between Runes and Wood

Wood is the most commonly used material for making runes. Although many other materials can be used, including stone, shells, bones, and paper, wood remains the highly used material. This is, however, not just a mere coincidence, but it is attributable to many facts about wood in runes mythology.

In all honesty, wood has great importance and is treated as a sacred element in rune mythology.

Two reasons can explain the importance of wood in rune mythology. The first one is the fact that the universe is structured in a way that looks like a tree. More specifically, a sacred tree by the name Yggdrasil is the one that holds everything in the world. It is believed that all other worlds hang from its branches. From the perspective of Norse mythology, nine worlds are brought together by the sacred tree. The nine worlds are:

Asgard: the heaven of gods

Muspellheim: the land of fire

Midgard: the land of human beings

Nifelheim: the land of ice

Jotunheim: the land of giants

Helheim: the land of the dead

Svartalfheim: the land of spirits of the night

Ljosalfheim: the land of the spirits of light

Vanaheim: the land of the spirits of water

Generally, as already said, all these nine worlds are held together by a tree, and hence, that explains why wood is a very vital material for runes. In the past, runes used to be carved into wood and stones for sacred reasons. Things have, however, changed over time, and other materials these days are also used. The striking reality that shows that, indeed, times have changed is how runes are now in papers, especially among modern rune enthusiasts. Notwithstanding the changes and many developments that have altered the original runes, wood remains connected to runes. It remains the most common material for making runes, especially among communities that have tried their best to retain the original meaning of runes and how they are used.

Healing of the Wound and How Odin Learned the 18 Chants

Having braced the cold and hurt himself to learn the secrets of runes, Odin took another step to learn more and more from the world of spirits. He climbed the Yggdrasil tree that holds the worlds. He got to the top, and after three days, the serious wounds he had started to heal by itself without Odin doing anything to aid the healing. It is believed that apart from getting the healing, Odin also learned a couple of other important secrets that he later spread to the world.

The number nine in rune mythology has great significance, and it was also used greatly while Odin was still in the tree. After staying there for nine days and nine nights, when he was almost to die, he had a strange voice. Two women were chanting as they engraved runes on pieces of wood. Hearing the sweet songs, Odin joined them and also started to recite the nine chants. The chants were, however, not to accompany the engraving of runes into woods, but they also served other different purposes. According to runic mythology, the nine chants helped Odin in the following ways:

- Protect him from any danger

- Put out fires

- Protect against the painful wounds

- Protect him against the right ropes

- Stop the spear in the fight

- Make sadness go away

- Stop any storm

- Protect against arrows

- Call upon the death of his enemy

The first nine chants were essentially for protection against the nine different perils already highlighted. After the first nine chants, nine others followed. These next nine were for resurrecting the god who died by hanging, making the giants to go away, calling the sun to rise, stealing the heart of a beautiful girl, stealing a woman's love, bring the happiness to a newborn baby, stop the witch in flight and to protect the friend in battle by making him invincible. After all these, Odin changed the 18th powerful one. It was, in fact, the strongest chant, but he never revealed it to anyone. It is said that Odin escaped when he chanted the 18th one, and that is how he survived the death he had seen approaching him.

The rope that Odin had used to tie himself to hang from the tree was removed, and as he fell on the ground, he got the nine initial pieces of wood that had runes engraved on them. He took them together with the new knowledge he acquired and later imparted it on humans. This process and time away in the cold region hanging on a tree is what is said to be the beginning of the story of runes. In his knowledge and wisdom, Odin increased the runes to 24 and revealed vital information about it to humans. The knowledge has since been handed down from one generation to another to date.

Secret Knowledge of Three Gods

The story of the three gods explains how the world was created by the three gods who worked together to bring life and new things to the new world. But even before delving into the process of creating the world and its components, there are lots of interesting facts about the first inhabitants of the world. More specifically, it is interesting to note that some came into being through unique natural processes.

According to rune mythology, a mixture of black poisoned ice and fire is what gave birth to Ymer. Another mixture of fire and clear ice is what gave birth to Audhulma. It is further written in runic books that Audhulma licked some blocks of ice to give birth to Bure. Bure had a son that was called Bur, who married Bestla. They together had three children who are the three great gods of the world, namely Odin, Vile, and Ve. These are the three gods that created the world and passed on the knowledge of runes.

The three gods killed Ymer and used his body to create the world. Each god took a piece or part of Ymer's body, and they together used it to create the world by makings hills, mountains, and plains from Ymer's body. Besides, the blood from his body was used to form the oceans, seas, and rivers.

Also, from runic mythology, the hair from Ymer's body formed the forests. All other features or components of the world were all created from the body parts of Ymer, who was killed by the three gods.

After creating the world and it was beautiful with flowing rivers and good-looking mountains, the three gods who created it gave it different parties. The land that had eyebrows surrounding it was given to humans to live in and use it. The land that had water surrounding was given by the gods to the giants. To sustain the sky and make the world safe, the three gods used four dwarfs, namely Soder, Vaster, Norr, and Oster, to sustain it in its rightful place.

How Humanity Came Into the Newly Created World

The three gods who took part in the creation of the world are also the same gods who are behind the beginning and appearance of humanity. It is said that one evening, while Odin and his two brothers were taking a walk, they came across two logs that caught their attention. They stopped for a while to have a look at the logs and see what could be done with them. It is said that Odin saw the shadows of his two brothers cast on the two logs, and he decided to breathe life into the two shadows on the logs. One log, specifically the ash one became a man. On the other hand, the other log by the name elm became the woman.

After Odin created the first two humans from the logs, the other gods also participated in the creation process by improving their characters. Ve is said to have given them the power of speech or the ability to communicate with each other. Vile, on the other hand, also gave them senses to help in their interaction. He also endowed them with judgment or the ability to make a decision when faced with a situation where one has to decide something or arrive at a conclusion based on the situation or issues at hand. From the first two humans, the world then increased, and the population grew as time went by. The three gods continued to help humans by giving them knowledge and wisdom of runes to assist them in uncovering daily hidden realities.

A Wrap Up of the Secrets

Indeed, there are lots of interesting kinds of stuff worth exploring the secrets of rune mythology and how the runes were handed down from Odin to other people in the world. All the happenings right from the time Odin was away in the cold region where he received the 18 chants to when humans were created took quite some time. The world has since developed, and it is believed that Odin, the god, and the inventor of runes still has his control over his people and those who keep using the knowledge and wisdom of runes that he left.

Chapter Eleven: Uncomfortable Truths about Norse Mythology

It goes without any saying that Norse Mythology has a lot of interesting facts. As a reader or student of it, you probably have learned a lot about it. To date, it remains one of the most popular mythos owing to its uniqueness and richness. The days of the week are named after the gods as well as goddesses of Nordic Mythos. In this chapter, we take you through another side of this mythology. You'll realize that, indeed, there are lots of things that many books written about runes do not tell you.

Apart from the many good things that many of us know about runes, there is a dark side that is rarely published or taught by runic teachers. Some episodes and uncomfortable truths about runic myths can spark your sixth sense and a desire to learn more about it. Very few people are aware of this since most stories written or taught about Norse Mythology often focus on the good side, leaving some other facts, yet they are also worth exploring. Although there is a lot, we have picked just ten to give you the true picture of the other side of Norse Mythology:

#1: Loki and the Horse

Something that many books and authors do not reveal is the strange love affair between Loki and a horse. It is said that after creating the world, the gods needed a home of their own where they would enjoy their time away from the world. They, therefore, built a kingdom and called it Asgard. Among the gods who lived there was Loki, a trickster god who was in between god and evil. He was the son of a giant god who spent most of his time helping Thor and Odin. He was not bad, but along the way, something unusual happened that most books do not report since it could potentially taint the image of gods.

It is believed that somewhere while with the gods in Asgard, Loki made love to a horse, and the act made the gods hostile to him. They even threatened him with cruel death not only for his affair with the horse but also for other issues he had with the gods in their home. He, therefore, went away with the horse and spent nine months of pregnancy together in one nest. He continued sharing his love with the horse, and after the period, he returned to the gods with an eight-legged horse baby. While there is a lot written about the home of gods and those who lived there, not many books expose this uncomfortable truth about some gods like Loki.

#2: The Incredibly Delicious Boar

Saehrímir, one of the Norse gods, was not an ordinary member of the kingdom of gods. He had a special role to play that no one else would in his absence. He was the god or boar cursed with immortality and the ability to get delicious. He had no end, and no even the presence of many people to be fed would threaten to bring him to an end.

Every morning, *Snorri,* the chef who took care of the needs of the members of the kingdom of gods, sliced off some pieces of flesh from *saehrími's* body. That was the order of every single day. Surprisingly, there is no day when food missed to be served in the kingdom even though there was only one supplier of the needed pieces of meat.

While many stories talk about the home gods and what they did while there, especially regarding the creation of humans, not all of them talk about *saehrímir*. He was a great member of the kingdom with a special role to play. Although his ability to grow and fill parts cut off from his body was seen as a curse, it appears that it was a blessing to the kingdom. However, not many books or stories written about Norse gods expose this interesting fact.

#3: Odin's Strict Adherence to All-Liquid Diet

It is said that there was a time when saehrímir, the boar grew bigger and tastier than ever in the past. The gods, therefore, decided to chop off more parts of the body than ever before and enjoyed the meal. All other Norse gods enjoyed the meat except Odin. However, Odin did not take it not because it was not served to him, but it is because he always ensured that his principles are adhered to without any deviation. He always insisted on taking his all-liquid diet.

Odin took his share of the meat and threw it to the dogs. He did not need for since, to him, the wine was both a drink as well as food. However, there was something strange about saehrímir's meat. He was never allowed to die even when a chunk of flesh was taken away as food from his body by the goods. Every time a section of his body was cut off, it would rapidly grow again and make the boar look okay with no missing parts of his body.

History has it that there was a time when chef Snorri decided to cut down the boar to his bone and removed almost all parts to the extent that no one would imagine that he would live again. To his surprise, the chef watched saehrímir's flesh grow again to its full status. On all these occasions, Odin never joined his fellow gods in enjoying the meat from the boar. He always made sure that he stuck to his liquid diet, and any meat is given to him finally ended to his dogs that were at all times waiting to feast on it.

#4: Odin's Wife Cheated on Him

One of the strangest stories you will not easily find in many books about Norse Mythology is the fact that Frigg, the wife of Odin, slept around with other gods. According to stories from ancient legends, there was a time when Odin went on a trip and delayed to come back home. His wife, by the name Frigg, assumed that Odin was probably dead or had been killed somewhere while he was away. She, therefore, quickly made up her mind that it was time to start having extra-marital affairs with other gods.

When Frigg could not wait any longer, she decided to give out Odin's possession to his brothers, Vili and Ve. The two gods took turns in sleeping with her, not knowing that Odin was on his way back home. The story does not, however, explain how Odin arrived home and whether he found the on the act. What is only explained is the fact that Frigg did not manage to keep her faithfulness to her husband while he was away.

The story is not only uncomfortable for a highly regarded Norse god, Odin, but it also raises other questions about Frigg and the powers associated with her. Some stories talk about Frigg's gift of prophecy. If at all she had it, then maybe it was not always strong at all times since she would have used it to know that Odin was not dead. She quickly decided to sleep around only to end up embarrassing his husband and his brothers, who took turns in making love to her while Odin was away.

#5: Odin Did Nothing to His Brothers Who Stole His Wife

One would have expected something terrible to happen when Odin arrived home and found that his brothers had taken away his possessions, including the wife. The whole affair simply ended without anything strange happening. Odin took back his possession, and that was the end of the story. There is nothing mentioned about his reaction or anything he did to Frigg or his brothers for taking away his share while he was away.

Odin did not seem to have been even miffed up by the awkward and embarrassing situation occasioned by his absence for a while. Moreover, he did not learn any lessons from happening since his behavior did not change much. Life went on as usual, as though nothing happened. It is not known whether the aftermath was not recorded or if it's true that the tale ended on an anticlimax note. With that said, the whole affair and how Odin behaved on his arrival back home is something that is not exposed in the Norse mythology.

#6: Baldur's Death

Odin had a second son called Baldur. From the time he was born, lots of good things were said about him. He had always been praised as the best and brightest son of Odin. Well, while that was the case for a long time, there is something else that is not often disclosed about him in the Norse mythology. They only say that he was a great and great son of Odin, but something worth knowing is hidden about him.

His destiny had been prophesied long ago, in fact, immediately from the time he was born. His character was all known, and his death had also been foreseen. He would die, and his death wasn't going to be a normal one. His death would mean the end of the world or what was known in runic language as Ragnarok, meaning the end of the world. However, Nordic stories do not reveal why he was regarded as the best son, yet contrary to the expectation, his death would again mean the end of the world. That is also another truth that is not put plainly in many books and tales about Norse gods and their lives.

#7: A Big Snake Holds the World Together

From the story of the creation of the world, it is said that the world is held together by the branches of a tree. There is also another version of the story that alleges that love is what holds together the world. Well, these are the most common accounts given about how the world is held together. However, there is another reality that many books and stories about runes and Norse Mythology do not bring to the attention of readers.

One of Loki's monster children, a giant serpent by the name Jormungandr holds the world together. Nordic tales report that the giant snake was taken away from his mother and father since there was no way that the gods would allow a giant snake to live with them in the kingdom of gods, Asgard. He was, therefore, thrown away. He lives in the ocean and be bites his tail as he holds the Earth together while waiting for his turn to fight back.

It is further said that the big giant will one day strike the gods that threw him away from his parents and his place in the kingdom of the Norse gods. More specifically, his target is to strike hard on Thor, whom he hates a lot. Come the time of Ragnarok or the end of the world; it is believed that the giant snake will slay Thor. While this is an interesting tale, it remains concealed in many runic books. That could be the case since it departs from what is always said about the nine worlds as told by Odin and how they are held together.

#8: There is A Squirrel that Just Loves Gossip in the Tree of Life

From Norse tales, everything in the world exists in the tree of life, Yggdrasil. All creations, including animals, all have places in the tree. For instance, there is an eagle in the branches of the tree and other roots; there is a dragon. It is said that these two creatures hate each other a lot, although they live in different parts. Possibly, they might not have even met at one time. So what could be the cause of their hatred?

It is believed that the squirrel is the reason for all the hatred that exists between the eagle and the dragon. Squirrel loves to gossip, and he moves up and down the tree all the time, conveying information and views that each animal has towards the other. For instance, when the eagle says something nasty about the dragon, it's the squirrel that runs down to tell the dragon. He also does the same when the dragon at the root part of the tree utters something or insults the eagle.

Funny enough, there is a tale that the squirrel, also called Ratatosk, loves the gossip and the job he does so much that whenever it cools, he always makes sure that there is something to carry up or takedown. His behavior is what has contributed to the prolonged hatred between these two creatures, yet they live differently in different territories of the world. Indeed, this is an interesting story, but this fact has remained hidden for long.

#9: Domaldi, the Swedish King, Did Not Enjoy His Life

One would have expected that by being a legendary king, Domaldi must have enjoyed his life during his reign. Contrary to this, it is said that sometimes, being a king is not a ticket to happiness, and neither does it guarantee one quality life. But what would someone of his stature fail to enjoy life, and he was the king? Well, it is said that the circumstances that led to his rise to the position of being a king are the reasons behind is trouble during his reign and even until his death.

Domaldi became the king because his two brothers killed their father. Although it was not his plan to have his father killed for him to get the throne, the whole act was seen as a curse. Since it was not cleansed and he as the king did not even bother to appease the angry gods, his reign was marked with great sorrows that deprived him of happiness. Famine and plague were the major problems that he had to deal with all the time. His people starved, and there were desperate times when desperate measures had to be taken to salvage the situation. There times, even when human beings had to be sacrificed in a bid to reduce the intensity and frequency of adversities.

Despite the many terrible things that happened during the reign of Domaldi, many books tend to paint him as the greatest Swedish king. The fact, however, is that he was never a happy king until his death. One last thing that is not always reported is that his county only saw great times after Domaldi's blood had been splashed on the altar. That is the time when Sweden's fate changed for good and calamities that had tormented her people stopped. The year that followed the death of Domaldi saw excellent harvests, and that marked the changed from constant sorrows to happiness.

#10: Odin's Magic Was Considered Unmanly

Norse mythology promotes Odin as the most important god among all other gods. He is attributed to the development or invention of runes, among many other things. However, that is not all that ought to be disclosed about him. Many uncomfortable truths are often not said about this god. Although they may not be as scary as others already discussed, it is good for any student and anyone else interested in learning runes to know these facts.

The first disturbing thing about Odin is his tendency to hoard knowledge. This is contrary to what one would have expected of him, bearing in mind that he spent days away and even hurt himself to acquire wisdom and knowledge of runes. On acquiring it and surviving even when he had almost died, he continued to search for knowledge but never dispersed it all to his fellows and even to humans. It is said that he often sent his servants to go and collect as much information from the universe as possible. However, instead of disseminating it, he hoarded it and never wanted anyone to know all the secrets he had learned firsthand and even those relayed to him by his servants.

Some popular literature also asserts that Odin was an unpopular god and his cult did not widespread as much as is often said or praised in many writings. Moreover, the kind of magic that he practiced called seidr was considered unmanly.

Some literature and tales even go on to name him as the god of death and betrayal. He also had to stab himself to understand runes or the magical writings he taught to his people, but, of course, after hoarding some secrets or parts, he knew alone. From his act of stabbing himself, it is further said that any sacrifice made to him was killed in the same manner. The killings were also extended to some kings who were his subjects, especially those considered as failures.

Why These Truths Are Hidden in Norse Mythology

Reading books and tales about Nordic goes, and their lives reveal that most of these truths are hidden. Besides, only a few teachers and runic tales expose these facts that somehow tend to twist the story said about runic gods and their roles in creating the world and influencing the lives of human beings. It is not that most pieces of literature praise runes, but the striking reality is the fact that some of these facts are quite interesting, and they just depict the reality of human life and what happens when people interact.

Apart from these uncomfortable truths, runes and Norse mythology remain interesting to explore for anyone interested in acquiring facts and more knowledge about runes. It is also worth noting that these truths do not, in any way, change the effectiveness or usefulness of runes among enthusiasts. They remain useful in dealing with daily challenges and situations that are often hard to solve without help. We can thus say that these uncomfortable truths only serve as an eye-opener and a call to take a look at the other interesting side often not made public.

Chapter Twelve: Runes and Naming of the Seven Days of the Week

Origins of the names that are given to the days of the week are attached to and traced to different sources, including runes. If you have explored this topic in the past, you will agree with us that, indeed, there are many and misleading stories about the names given to the days of the week. In this chapter, we give you details of the link between these days and Norse mythology. Indeed, there is a close link and many Norse Runes associated with the days of the week.

Apart from the days of the week being named after runic gods, there are also rules regarding the best times to cast or draw some specific runes. It is, therefore, very vital to understand this as part of your journey to mastering runes. If you intend to be casting them as often as possible, then this is the section that you need to give a lot of emphasis to. Without further ado, here are the days of the week and the secret knowledge about the connection between these days and various runes:

Sunday

Sunday is named after the sun, and it is a symbol of life and creation as well as renewal. Today, many people view this day as an excellent day of social approval and activities. People attend parties, weddings, churches, short trips, and even rejuvenation. Also, promotions for health, wellness, and related activities are normally done on this day. All these activities are best suited for the day since it is a day of warmth and self-confidence.

SOWELU is the rune associated with Sunday. It is a symbol of energy and success; hence, it is a strong and powerful rune that is associated with many good things. If you want to use runes for prosperity and good, then the best day to cast your types are on Sunday since it is the day of good. Used well, SOWELU can help you get rid of negativity and sadness that could be affecting your life. It is this great to seek the true and real meaning of this day named after the sun as well as the rune of great achievement.

Monday

Monday means moon day or the body that wanes and moves the tides as well as reflects light from the sun. Based on its meaning, it is a day of quiet meditation, talking to friends and relatives. You can also use it to read, record your dreams, write a few things, and other related activities. The most important one here is to have quality time with your loved ones and especially family members.

LAGUZ is the rune associated with Monday. This rune is associated with rain, water, sea, and lakes, among other water or fluid bodies. In a nutshell, this rune is associated or used when one wants an intervention with seeking true value and meaning. The rune is also used or is an indication of the renewal of the land through rain and plenty of life. Water is life hence the association. You can give it a try, and you'll, indeed, enjoy renewal and newness in all your activities.

Tuesday

Tuesday is also called Tyr's day or the day of the god known to make great sacrifices for others and especially those who believe in him. He is also a great warrior but not for physical battles or those involving killings. Instead, he fights spiritual battles, and he has never been reported to have lost anywhere. Many people associate him with doing good causes or sacrificing for others to benefit. If you are a Tuesday person, you need a great heart. Most importantly, you need courage, self-conquest, and readiness to face fear and take calculated risks.

TEIWAZ is the rune that is associated with Tuesday. Rune readers and users often use it when they want leadership or mastery of something associated with a worthy cause. Tuesday is, therefore, a good day for doing fundraisings, seeking justice, resolving serious issues and other tasks geared towards helping others. People of goodwill and who understand runes often organize humanitarian activities on this day. Sport parades and military activities are also good for this day.

Wednesday

Odin features greatly in runic tales and Norse mythology for many amazing reasons and especially his role. Therefore, Wednesday is Woden's or Odin's day. He is the wise elder and the wisdom behind the runes. He wandered away in a cold region to look for an opportunity to drink from the spring of wisdom. He, however, had to endure pain to succeed and get new knowledge that he wanted. Finally, after days of suffering and hurting his body, he was able to get the 18 initial runes.

The rune associated with Wednesday is ANSUZ. In simple terms, ANSUZ is the staff of Odin who links up the Earth with Heaven. The appearance of this rune in your casting is a clear spiritual message of coming blessings. It is almost an element of a powerful surprise. For this reason, Wednesdays are the best for meetings, interviews, seminars, and workshops. Promotions and advertisements also fit this great day. Finally, film, music, and poetry are some of the things you can schedule to do on this big day of Odin.

Thursday

Thursday is Thor's day, the god who symbolizes great power, influence, and victory over any form of opposition. If you are facing fear and there is something that you seriously want to conquer, then this is the day you need to consider for your tasks. If you believe, have the courage and readiness, then you can easily strike like Thor or lightning to make it a bit clearer. Thor is known to motivate, especially at instances where one has to face fear.

Rune associated with Thursday is EHWAZ, the rune of movement. For this reason, Thursday is the best day for energetic drives. Some rune readers and teachers call it the day of the horse to imply that it is a day that is associated with great movements. It is a great day to declare your moves, plans, and innovative pursuits. It is time to work on those major projects that you have, and you need to triumph despite all odds.

Friday

Name after Frigg, the wife of Odin, Friday is generally a day of unity and relationship. It is all about giving, receiving, and engaging in activities of mutual benefits. If you plan to give someone a special gift, then the best day to do so is on Friday. It is also a day to unite and exercise mutual respect, especially with special parties. It is the day when people cement their loving relationships or make great business offers to their partners.

GEBO is the rune associated with Friday. The name of this rune means a gift hence explaining why this is a gift day. Based on this, some of the activities usually organized or carried out on this day include but are not limited to birthday outings, engagement parties, romantic dinners, dating, and other meetings. The day is also favorable for artistry, jewelry, and beauty works. It is, indeed, a great day for great times.

Saturday

Saturday stands for self-discipline, and it is a day that is named after Saturn. It is a day of duty and karmic obligation. More specifically, it is a day of rewards, although people no longer give it the seriousness it deserves as witnessed by the many and busy activities that people do on this day that would otherwise be of rest. In Hebrew, it is the Sabbath day or the day when God rested after finishing his works of creation. Some still observe it, and they keep it as a holy day to serve God and stay away from the usual heavy duties and tasks often carried out on other days.

JERA is the rune that is associated with Saturday. It implies harvest or guaranteed success after days of serious work. It is the cycle of a harvest that comes after planting and working hard to keep the plants good. Based on this, Saturdays are good for harvest celebrations, a graduation dinner, and traditional ceremonies. It is, therefore, a day that deserves those activities that require a serious tone but should not be taxing a lot when it comes to energy and time, as well.

As illustrated, all the days of the week are associated and named after different Norse gods and the different activities that they were known for during ancient times. Besides, each day has a rune that is associated with it. What this means is that when you cast or do a runic exercise and you get any of those that are related to the days of the week, the chances are that the outcome of the activity that you are pondering is related with the tasks and events highlighted as best suited for each of those days.

Are there Bad and Good Days?

From the discussion on the days of the week, it is not right to say that some days are bad or worse than others. As illustrated, there are different activities that one can do on any of the days of the week. Your decision on what to do should, therefore, be guided by the event that you are planning or the situation at hand. If you pick the right day, then you will, without any doubt, achieve the best. All events, according to the Nordic calendar and runes associated with the different days of the week, were chosen for specific reasons. Those should be your guidelines when making your calendar of events.

If you want to organize a birthday party, you now know which day best it suits. Weddings, harvests, gifting, doing charity work, resting, and all other events have days set aside for them based on the Nordic calendar and runes related to them. If you are a rune student or teacher, you now have a reason to reconsider how you plan events if you want to experience the joy and happiness that comes with following the runic calendar. Each day is best for something, and that is the most important thing to note.

Chapter Thirteen: Runes and the Power Plants' Flowers

Over the years, there has been an increase in the use of flowers to represent the different runes. It is not, therefore, surprising to find someone with 24 different plants with flowers that represent the runes and their associated properties. Although it is a practice that wasn't too widespread, its use began a long time ago, and it has improved over time with different runic enthusiasts giving it a new meaning altogether. However, unlike other plants grown in the garden, those associated with runes are unique in many ways. They are planted in specific places of the garden and in certain patterns depending on the runes that they represent. Indeed, great care has to be taken to stop the energies from clashing in the garden.

The idea of planting flowers in the garden with runic attachments is to bring out the desired life changes to help solve common problems that need runic intervention. It, therefore, follows that not all runic flowers should be grown in one garden. One can just concentrate on those that are of interest or can bring the desired change. Once the appropriate runes are chosen, they can be planted or placed in specific places of interest. For instance, some flowers can be grown in pots and placed near the bedside or any other place where runic energies are desired.

Runes and Their Corresponding Flowers

EOLH: Often used when seeking protection from enemies and evils that may be out to cause unexpected harm or any misfortune. It is also associated with luck, strength, and energies required to go about life activities. There is a plant that has these features, and it is often grown to represent this rune.

Flower: rush plant commonly grown in the east

SIGEL: rune often associated with healing, success, victory in a battle, clear thinking, and self-confidence. If these are the things you need in life, then you can plant a flower that is associated with this rune and its energies. Flower grown to represent this rune exhibits these features, and hence, it is chosen to represent this rune in the garden.

Flower: St John's wort grown in the east

TIR: rune of quick recuperation often used in times of trouble where quick recovery is desired. It also aids a lot when there are competitions, and victory is an important factor. It can be termed as rapid response rune in times of struggle and need for quick recovery or victory. Do you know a plant that has this feature? That's what is often grown to represent it.

Flower: red hot poker grown in the east

BEORC: rune often used to help when there are fertility issues, domestic problems, or family affairs that need intervention to resolve. Apart from being used when aid is needed in the family, this rune can also be used for protection against matters that threaten family life. If interested, you can choose to get wood with an inscription of this rune or grow a flower that has the features and the energies associated with this rune.

Flower: night-scented stock grown in the north

EOH: if you even experience transport problems and you need aid, then this is the rune you should try. It is normally used to bring swift and specific changes that one desires. Most importantly, all problems related to movement or transport can easily be solved by this run when used well. If you are traveling and you want something in your garden to remind you about this rune, then there is a flower you can plant.

Flower: forsythia grown in the north

FEOH: if you want an increase in wealth and all your property, then this is the rune you should consider using. It not only helps in increasing them, but it also helps in protecting all your valuables. In some instances, people also seek the help of this rune when they want to hasten things from one level to another. You can have a flower that reminds you if this great need and how you can move faster to get to the levels you desire.

Flower: lily of the valley grown in the south and also in the north

UR: want to initiate new circumstances into your life? UR is the rune to use. It is also useful in the maintenance of good health and protection from all kinds of health issues. Flowers planted to represent this rune are, therefore, those associated with new life and keeping of good health, especially in hard times. Similarly, and like the other runes, you can have a flower to represent the rune in your garden and what it can offer you.

Flower: nasturtium flower grown in the north

THORN: when this fall out of hand or turn out to be the opposite of what you expected, then the rune you can use is THORN. You can also use it when you need luck in your life or to overcome circumstances that are beyond your control. A flower in your garden can help you get these favors if you grow the right one and in the right place in your garden.

Flower: honesty plant grown in the south

ANSUR: often used to gain wisdom and especially the knowledge and courage that is needed for one to tackle an exam successfully. If you also want to master public speaking, communication, and related skills, then this is the rune you should consider using to get needs. Want a flower instead of the real rune? It's there, and you can try it.

Flower: morning glory plant is often grown in the south

RAD: used for safety in all travel means including planes, cars, bikes, buses, and trains among all others. It does not only facilitate safe travel, but it also provides comfort throughout the journey. You can thus use it if you need to travel by any of these means. It works, and many travelers often seek the aid of this rune.

Flower: snapdragon that's grown in the east

MANN: used when looking for assistance or to win goodwill from others. It is also generally helpful in group activities or any cause that is aimed at improving mankind. If you also want a boost in mental power, then this is the rune to consider. You can have a plant to remind you of this amazing runic power near you and especially in your garden.

Flower: foxglove plant grown in the east

ING: brings a sudden release of energy, and it is often used when a satisfactory conclusion is needed. It has also been used severally when there are fertility issues to be solved. It also fixes issues and helps in satisfactorily ending them. Instead of getting the rune itself, a flower in your garden can still do the same work.

Flower: gentian plant grown in the north or west

LAGU: do you have artistic endeavors, and you need help? This is the rune you can use to get what you want. It helps in creating inner awareness and boosting vital life-force energies. It also greatly helps intuition. What type of flower or plant can you grow to represent this rune at home? Here's it.

Flower: water lily plant that is grown in the west

OTHEL: used in protecting the land, house, and all other possessions, including long-term investments. One can also use it when asking for good health for the elderly and good co-existence among people. It encourages humility and respect for one another.

Flower: snowdrop plant grown in the south or the east

DAEG: struggling to change attitude, but it is becoming a bit challenging? This is the rune you should consider giving a try. It can help you change your attitude, so you completely take a new direction altogether and renounce any paths that you are not okay with. It is also used in re-evaluations and when you want an increase in finances.

Flower: marigold plant often grown in the north

GEOFU: sex, love, and anything involving partnerships between people of the opposite gender can be aided by this rune. If you also happen to have lost mental stability and you would like to restore equilibrium, then this is the rune you should consider using. The flower associated with it is also believed to have energies related to these areas.

Flower: lad's love plant grown in the east

WYNN: if you love your career and you want to bring fulfillment in it, then this rune can help you achieve that goal. Some runic enthusiasts also use it for success in their travels or adventures, especially to places unknown to them. It, however, works well in the area of career development and fulfillment.

Flower: larkspur plant grown in the north

KEN: used for stability of love and when seeking a fresh start after a happening. If you also need to boost your passion in a relationship, then this is the rune to use. The plant that is associated with it is, therefore, associated with this kind of problem and human needs, including healing.

Flower: wild rose grown in the south

HAGALL: this rune is used for protection, and also when one is venturing in a gambling situation where luck is needed. If these are the things you need, then you should consider using this rune. The flower associated with it is known to have a feature and scent that relates to these needs.

Flower: fern plant grown in the south

PEORTH: this rune is used when searching for lots of things that have become a little bit hard to trace. It also helps with all sorts of psychological problems that one could be facing and need immediate help. Finally, it promotes mental health and healing. There is a plant that has been selected to represent these properties, and you can have it in your home.

Flower: chrysanthemum plant grown in the west

JARA: this rune is used when one desires tangible results or an outcome from a situation. More specifically, it is applicable when you put in effort, money, or time, and you want something great out of it. Also, people often call this rune when they need help in legal matters that are a bit challenging or can easily change one's life. You can plant a flower and successfully bring these changes or help in your life.

Flower: the cornflower plant is grown in the north

IS: you've probably heard of the association between this rune and sweet pea. Indeed, this rune is used for sweet causes or in freezing things or when there is a need to halt undesirable forces. Also, the flowers often planted to represent this rune, and its energies have a characteristic feature of these needs.

Flower: sweet pea that's grown in the west

YR: if you are facing so many obstacles and you do not know how you can remove them, then this rune can help you fix them. It not only removes obstacles, but it can also help you turn them into stepping stones to the level of success that you desire to achieve. You can also use it when you want more power to help you overcome the challenges that you are facing. The flower often has grown to represent this rune, too, has these features.

Flower: a lilac plant that's often grown anywhere

NIED: if you have long-term goals and achieving them is becoming a bit difficult, then you can use this rune to achieve them. NIED helps aid in causes that take long, such as a long search for a lover or when one has a relationship that has stood for years and needs to be spiced up to keep it alive. The flower associated with it represents these energies.

Flower: crocus plant grown in the south

The idea of using plants or flowers to represent runic properties is, indeed, a reality in many places where runes are valued and used to help in meeting daily needs. It is, however, good to know which plants represent which runes and where can you appropriately grow them at home, so you enjoy their benefits. You can only enjoy the energies if you plant the right flowers and, most importantly, in the right places in your garden or other places that you choose.

Chapter Fourteen: Going Deeper

Thinking about taking up a course in runes? Well, learning it, especially with no prior experience in it, requires a clear approach, especially if you want to master it in the shortest time possible. Also, while learning on your own can be the best option, there are a couple of things you need to know first before you can start your classes. Most importantly, you need to find a way that will make it easy for you to master it and apply it correctly, like the runic natives.

Why Learn Runes?

Even before delving into the effective techniques of learning runes, you would ask yourself why you need it in the first place. Having good reasons before you start will propel you to take up the challenge and be a runemaster sooner or later. Your motivation to learn runes will also determine the best approach that you can use to learn runes. Away from that, here are great reasons why you may want to learn runes if you already do not know this ancient practice that has stood the test of time:

- **To Get Pieces of Advice Regarding Life**

In life, everyone is often faced with situations where making a decision can be a bit challenging. In such instances, having a method that helps you make a prediction is great as it helps you save time as well as get the best advice. Besides, life is not all about making such a decision. You should also have a basis for every decision that you make.

Runes are a great tool that can aid in decision making if used well. You can use them to get advice as well as the best way forward when you are faced with a situation where you need quick help. More specifically, runes can advise you on matters of friendship, relationship, love, business, next move, and many other areas. You simply need to learn how you can use them to get a piece of advice on anything that could be giving you a headache.

- **For Protection against Negative Influences**

It's been said many times that the world is full of negative influence, evil, curses, and many other things that tend to affect human life negatively. Some of these happenings occur openly, while others can be things that are secretly being tested and directed towards your life without your knowledge. One, therefore, needs a way of protection against all these vices since their effects can be severe and with far-reaching consequences.

Runes can be used for protection as many of them are associated with protection and have been used ever since their invention with amazing testimonies of their effectiveness. More specifically, there are powerful runic talismans that not only offer protection but can also help you attract good to your life. You can thus learn runes for this purpose, especially if you feel that your life is a bit not heading in the right direction due to negative influences.

- **To Foretell the Future**

If there was a way of uncovering what is likely to happen in the future, everyone would no doubt want to know what the future holds for them. While it cannot be possible to expose what is going to happen completely, there are ways in which one can use to get a rough idea of what is most likely to happen. Some runes and castings can be used for this purpose if you really what to make a reliable prediction about your future. You may, therefore, want to learn runes for this specific task of exploring the likelihood of the future.

- **Just for Fun**

Learning Norse Mythology can be fun, especially if you can relate and compare what you learn with what other myths have to say about the world. Some aspects of runic language, its invention, stories about the runic gods, and many other topics can be entertaining. Many people learn runes for this purpose. You, too, can join them by exploring the interesting facts about Odin and how the world came into being.

You should, however, note that learning runes for fun should be approached in a way that is interesting and fun as opposed to when learning it for use. Most importantly, your course should focus on the interesting parts only without having to venture into the technical areas that sometimes seem to be hard. Precisely, your reading and learning should be fun throughout without anything technical.

- **Intellectual Joy of Learning a New Thing**

Runes are powerful magical symbols that, if you successfully learn how to use them, you are most likely to experience some kind of joy. People take several months and even years in some cases to master runes completely. If you are sharp enough to complete the job on time and master it, you will no doubt feel that you've accomplished something that some people often take a long time to accomplish.

For people who are not from Europe, learning runes and how to use them can be a chance to have a taste of western mythologies. For instance, runic alphabets differ from those used in English and other languages. As a result, exploring it can help you appreciate the differences that exist between them and the possible reasons behind the difference. All these are not simple tasks to do, but if one successfully takes runic classes, that in no doubt amounts to a big achievement.

Any Prerequisites

You do not need any prerequisites to take up a course in runes successfully. All you need is a ready mind and the preparedness to learn new things. Although prior experience is always an added advantage to any student, no proof that is not having it is going to make it impossible for you. You just need to know that you are exploring something that is quite extensive and with different explanations of things you possibly already know.

The Most Effective Ways to Learn Runes

Unlike in the past, when one had to attend class physically, these days, there are effective methods that one can use to learn runes. It doesn't matter your location or background. Most of these methods are easy, and anyone can use them effectively to learn runes. Without further ado, here are some ways that you can consider:

Online Classes

With the growing internet of things, you can easily and without any hassle effectively take online classes on runes. All you need is an internet-enabled device and readiness to enroll with a reliable provider of runic courses and start as soon as you can to take up the classes. This method works well, especially if you have other commitments that limit you to specific free times only. With online classes, you do not have to stick to any time since they give you the convenience and flexibility that you need to be successful.

You may, however, need to exercise some bit of care with online classes since there are many providers out there, and choosing a few from them can be an uphill task. The best way to pick the best is to take the time to assess their course, how long they have offered it, and what other students have to say about it. That will help you get the right picture of whether the online provider you are considering is the best among your many options.

Buy a Book and Read on Your Own

If you want to just enjoy full convenience without even using the internet, then your other option of learning runes can be buying and reading books about it. With this option, you do not even need an internet-enabled device. You just need to acquire the right books, and you are set to continue learning your stuff. Provided you have the right books and other materials, learning runes can be simple, especially if you are sharp enough to grasp concepts without explanations or tutorials.

One thing worth noting about reading on your own is that you need first to make sure that your resources are the right ones. Today, a simple search on the internet on some of the best runic books brings a lot of options. If you want reliable ones that are of good quality, then purchase from leading platforms known for quality products and great customer care. Most importantly, find out what other readers of the books you are considering have to say about it.

Hire a Friend or a Known Runic Teacher

If you have someone near you that you are sure is a master of runes and can guide you through the process, then that can also be another great option. Many people have learned runes, and some have mastered the art and are ready to help those learning it. If you are lucky to have some in your place, then you can use them to teach you Norse Mythology, and the art of using runes for different purposes.

Having your runic teacher, especially who loves the job and knows what it takes to master it is the best option successfully.

It makes learning real, and you are more likely to move faster as opposed to learning alone. You should, however, be careful to make sure that the person you are hiring understands as many aspects of runes as possible. Also, get someone who is interested in the topic and does not incline towards any side, especially when it comes to some Norse tales and myths.

Join Groups that Teach Runes

Groups do exist that teach runes, and that too is an option that you can explore if you are interested in learning and mastering runes. In European and especially Germany and other counties, there are groups that even practice group casting and other runic practices. If you are in any of these areas or other places where such groups exist, then that is a great way to realize your dream of being a runemaster.

When you join a group, the likelihood of mastering runes faster increases since you are more likely to compete with peers or be encouraged by their moves, it is, therefore, one of the most effective ways to learn runes and put into practice the concepts that you learn. Also, working alone can be tough, especially when it gets to the technical aspects of the course. That can, however, change if you approach the work as a group, so you share ideas on how to go about any challenging areas.

Watch Videos and Tutorials about Runes

With the increased demand for runic lessons, some teachers have developed methods that use videos to teach runes and related stuff. This is, therefore, one of the ways that you can use to learn runes. It is effective in the sense that you see what to do right from the introduction to the end. If you search online, you will find a couple of videos that are related to runes. Some sites also provide tutorials on runes to interested learners who would like to understand what runes mean and how they can be used in day to day living. If you pick a couple of them or just a few that are reliable, then you are likely to master the topic.

One great advantage of videos and online tutorials is the fact that you get to see exactly what you are supposed to do, especially when it comes to exercises. It is a method that works, and many people have applied and are now serious users of runes in their daily living activities. Some are free, while others are for a subscription. What is important for you is to choose the best, so you learn easily and without taking too long. Provided you have the best and especially those don in the language that you understand, you are going to eventually understand how runes work and how you can use them for different purposes.

Not Sure If You Need a Class or Runic Teacher

As you have seen from the subsections above, there are many great reasons why learning runes is a good experience. Most importantly, you now know some of the most effective ways that you can use to make learning easy. It can still be a difficult task to make a decision even with the great information provided here. So what can you do in such a situation of indifference or indecision? It is better to seek advice. You probably need one more reason to start the journey to learning runes and even using them.

As a way of concluding this chapter, it is great to bring to your attention that Norse runes can help you experience a wonderful sense of empowerment to take your everyday activities. Using them, especially to connect with nature, can be uplifting. It can be the only support you eventually need to experience a breakthrough in life. As already highlighted, there are many amazing reasons to take up rune classes and learn how these ancient practices can be applied for different purposes in your daily life.

Experimenting and testing it before actually getting deeper into it can also be a motivation. Some things may just sound good, but without a taste or picture of what it is to use them, one can doubt whether there is any need even to start learning them. If you want a taste, learn the simple ones and give it a try. If it works and you enjoy the experience, go ahead to apply them as much as you want. With that said, there is, indeed, evidence that learning runes are a great thing if you have been thinking about it but haven't gotten a chance to start the learning process.

Conclusion

Runes have been of great importance not only to the Germanic people but also to others in different parts of the world who have over time learned runes. Although a lot has changed regarding the practice of runes, the fact remains that they hold a dear place in many people's hearts. They are used for spell casting, divination, seeing the future, and connecting to nature and the spirit world. While most of these are ancient practices, runes still have a role to play in the modern-day society. That's why there are tremendous improvements in runic language, signs, and exercises to accompany the learning process.

Contrary to the many misconceptions that have been peddled for years about runes, it is a fascinating topic. There are many people who understand what runes and activities related to it are all about. They have thus invested in learning and perfecting thins like rune casting, rune exercises and interpreting signs, divination, and other interesting stuff to explore about runes. Others, as shown in the book, even write poems about runes to describe the various runic signs and connect with them. All these and many other efforts not discussed are a clear indication that runes have an important place in the daily lives of those who know the amazing benefits of runes.

The goal of this book was to simplify the process of learning runes and make it interesting to anyone interested in them. Most importantly, it has explained what runes are, their history, origin, gods, and goddesses associated with them and the evolution of the runic alphabet to its current status. Indeed, there is a lot to learn about runes and their place in the ever-changing world. As we come to the end of this book, we hope that this book has helped you learn the amazing things you probably did not know about runes.

Thank you for taking the time to read the book. What did you think of, **Runes: A Guide To The Magic, Meanings, Spells, Divination & Rituals Of Runes**

I know you could have picked any number of books to read, but you picked this book and for that I am extremely grateful. I hope that it added at value and quality to your everyday life. If so, it would be really nice if you could share this book with your friends and family by posting to Facebook and Twitter.

If you enjoyed this book and found some benefit in reading this, I'd like to hear from you and hope that you could take some time to post a review. I want you, the reader, to know that your review is very important and so, if you'd like to leave a review, all you have to do is click here and away you go. I wish you all the best in your future success!

Thank you and good luck!

Sofia Visconti 2019

Resources

Antonsen, E. H. (2011). *Runes and Germanic linguistics* (Vol. 140). Walter de Gruyter.

Barnes, M. P. (2012). *Runes: a handbook*. Boydell Press.

Blum, R. (1983). *The Book of Runes: A Handbook for the Use of an Ancient Oracle.*

Farnell, K. (2006). *Simply Runes*

Holmes, K. (2013). *Pagan Portals: Runes.*

Imer, L. (2010). Runes and Romans in the North. *Futhark: International Journal of Runic Studies, 1*, 41-64.

Joseph, F. (2010). *Gods of the Runes: The Divine Shapers of Fate*. Simon and Schuster.

Krasskova, G. (2010). *Runes: Theory & Practice*. New Page Books.

MOUNTFORT, P. (2015). Rune casting: Runic Guidebooks as Gothic Literature and the Other Gothic Revival. *Popular Gothic*, 16.

Page, R. I. (2006). *An introduction to English runes*. Boydell Press.

Paxson, D. L. (2005). *Taking Up the Runes: A Complete Guide to Using Runes in Spells, Rituals, Divination, and Magic*. Weiser Books.

Peschel, L. (1989). *A Practical Guide to the Runes: Their Uses in Divination and Magick*. Llewellyn Worldwide.

Robertson, J. S. (2012). How the Germanic futhark came from the Roman alphabet. *Futhark: International Journal of Runic Studies*, 2, 7-26.

Saille, H. (2009). *The Spiritual Runes: A Guide to the Ancestral Wisdom*. O Books.

CLAIM THIS NOW

Discover the Ancient Healing Power of Reiki, Awaken Your Mind, Body, Spirit and Heal Your Life

Reiki has the power to heal our minds, bodies, and spirits in ways few of us can imagine.

This is applicable to individuals of any age with physical, mental, emotional, or even spiritual problems. For many years Reiki has been a highly guarded secret but it is intelligent energy, which automatically goes to where it is needed.

Find out more in this complete guide to an ancient healing art to living a happier, healthier, and better life.

www.ingramcontent.com/pod-product-compliance
Lightning Source LLC
Chambersburg PA
CBHW021110080526
44587CB00010B/466